à *Jean-Paul*

CHAMONIX

HORS-PISTES
OFF-PISTE

Jean-Paul LASSALLE était un skieur d'instinct. Sa descente du couloir de la Table à l'Aiguille du Tour - en trace directe! - est tombée dans l'oubli, trop rapide pour laisser une trace.

Parlant du ski hors-piste, il disait: "c'est comme quitter le bitume pour aller sur la pelouse."

Le 28 mars 1980 ses mots et ses gestes se sont tus, endormis sous la neige.

Jean-Paul LASSALLE was an instinctive skier. His descent of the couloir de la Table - straight down - is a forgotten action, too fast to leave a trace.

Talking about off-piste he said that, "its like leaving the tarmac to drive off-road".

The 28 March 1980 his words and his deeds fell silent, asleep under the snow.

CHAMONIX

HORS-PISTES
OFF-PISTE

François BURNIER
Dominique POTARD

guides de haute montagne

Traduction de
Murray BALL

guide de haute montagne

Le Vieux Servoz - 74310 SERVOZ - FRANCE

Des mêmes auteurs / *By the same authors*:

"Guide des écoles d'escalade de la vallée de Chamonix"
"Escalades en Espagne / *Climbing in Spain*"
"Mont-Blanc, courses faciles"
"Escalades en Thaïlande / *Climbing in Thailand*"

Photos de couverture
Cover Photos: René ROBERT

Imprimé en Italie
© Editions **VAMOS, 2001**
   www.editionsvamos.com
Imprimerie MARCOZ s. n. c. - Place E. Chanoux, 1
11017 Morgex - Vallée d'Aoste (Italie) - Tél. 0165.809640
Tous droits de traduction et de reproduction réservés pour tous pays.
Dessins de Dominique POTARD, sauf pages 126 et 127.

I.S.S.N.: 1159-9413
I.S.B.N.: 2-910672-10-7
Dépôt légal: janvier 2001

Nous sommes heureux de remercier ici, pour leur agréable concours:
- Murray BALL, guide et traducteur.
- Tim BARNETT, photographe.
- Paul BERGUERAND, moniteur de ski.
- Jacques BERNY, photographe.
- Philippe BIDAULT, guide.
- Jean BRISSAUD, ex-directeur de l'Office du Tourisme de Chamonix.
- Jean-Marc BONINO, Directeur du Service Juridique et de l'Aménagement de la Commune de Chamonix.
- Neil BRODIE, traducteur.
- Thierry CHARLET (et Barinda), Adjoint au Chef d'Exploitation de Balme.
- Louis FOLLIGUET, Directeur des Remontées Mécaniques du Brévent.
- Florence LASSERRE.
- Nicole LEHMANN, traductrice.
- Jean-Pierre MANSART, guide.
- Jean-Claude MARRO, ex-directeur des Remontées Mécaniques de la Flègère.
- Martial MOIOLI, One Sport.
- Xavier MURILLO, photographe.
- Jean-Claude PILLOT, dit "Manet", guide.
- Arnaud PINGUET, Secrétaire Général du Conseil Supérieur des Sports de Montagne.
- André POLLET-VILLARD, de la Société Touristique du Mont-Blanc.
- Bernard PRUDHOMME, directeur de l'Office du Tourisme de Chamonix.
- Bernard RAVANEL, ex-chef des Pistes de Lognan - Les Grands Montets.
- Brian RAWCLIFFE, traducteur.
- René ROBERT, photographe.

ainsi que:
- L'Association Nationale pour l'Etude de la Neige et des Avalanches (A.N.E.N.A.).
- Le Peloton de Gendarmerie de Haute Montagne, de Chamonix (P.G.H.M.).
- L'Association "Les Campanules".

Les rapports du public et du ski hors-pistes semblent échapper à toute objectivité. Si le sauvetage héliporté d'un skieur évoluant hors des sentiers battus met en émoi toute la station, les accidents quotidiens survenant sur le domaine sécurisé passent quasiment inaperçus; il est vrai que le traîneau fait malheureusement partie de l'environnement et du folklore du grand cirque blanc.

Hors des pistes en revanche, l'accident n'apparaît que comme la sanction inévitable, et légitime, pour ces inconscients qui osent braver les appels à la prudence.

Parallèlement des dizaines de films projetés dans les vidéo-bars, émissions "aventures", et autres festivals de la Glisse, gavent les adolescents d'images de virtuoses jouant avec la poudreuse, surfant les avalanches... représentation idyllique où les dangers de la neige ne sont plus jamais évoqués.

Entre ces deux extrêmes, nous croyons qu'il existe un juste équilibre; celui d'une pratique responsable faite de respect et de connaissance de la montagne.

Terre de liberté, l'altitude est un espace sauvage, qu'il faut apprendre à connaître, tout en sachant qu'il nous échappera toujours quelque chose.

Puisse ce petit livre contribuer à cette connaissance, sans trahir l'éthique des gens du pays, alliage d'humilité et de sagesse.

Les éditeurs

The public view of off-piste skiing seems to escape all objectivity. If the helicopter rescue of an injured skier, who has strayed a little off the beaten track puts in a flutter the whole station, the daily accidents which happen on the patrolled domaine pass almost unnoticed; it's true however, that the "blood-wagon" is an inextricable part of the folklore surrounding the big white circus. On the other hand, off-piste accidents appear as unavoidable, even legitimate for those inconsequential souls ignoring the calls for prudence.

Parellel to this, the films projected in video-bars, mountain-film festivals and other "adrenalin" programs, bombard adolescents with images of "virtuosos" playing in the powder, or surfing down avalanches... an idyllic representation where the dangers that the snow hides are never alluded to.

Between these two extremes there is a balance, that of a responsible approach, coming from respect and knowledge of the mountains.

At altitude there exists another environment, wild, one that takes time to understand, at the same time realising that one can never know it all...

May this small book contribute to this knowledge, without betraying the mountain people ethic, a blend of humility and wisdom.

The Editors

◇

1ère partie

VERS UNE PRATIQUE RESPONSABLE DU SKI HORS-PISTES

Part one

TOWARDS RESPONSIBLE OFF-PISTE SKIING

UN PEU DE VOCABULAIRE

- **Adret**: versant ensoleillé d'une vallée (opposé à l'ubac)
- **Amont**: côté montagne (en opposition à l'aval).
- **Arête**: partie plus ou moins saillante d'une montagne, séparant deux versants.
- **A.R.V.A**: Appareil de Recherche des Victimes d'Avalanches, sous forme d'un petit émetteur-récepteur individuel.
- **Aval**: côté vallée.
- **Balisage**: système de signalisation des pistes.
- **Balisage central**: les piquets jalonnent le milieu de la piste.
- **Balisage latéral**: les piquets bordent la piste.
- **Barre**: barrière de rocher ou de glace.
- **Baudrier**: sorte de harnais pour l'alpinisme offrant un meilleur confort en cas de suspension.
- **Botter**: verbe indiquant que la neige colle sous les skis ou les crampons.
- **Calotte**: masse glaciaire arrondie pouvant coiffer un sommet.
- **Combe**: petite vallée en auge.
- **Contrepente**: flanc d'un couloir ou d'une combe.
- **Coulée**: petite avalanche.
- **Couloir**: passage plus ou moins étroit entre deux parois.
- **Corniche**: surplomb de neige formé par le vent sur une crête.
- **Corps mort**: tout objet (ski, bâton...) enfoui dans la neige pour servir d'ancrage.
- **Crevasse**: fracture d'un glacier.
- **Dévissage**: chute pour un skieur ou un alpiniste.
- **Exposé**: se dit d'un passage dangereux.
- **Face**: versant d'une montagne.
- **Gendarme**: proéminence isolée d'une arête.
- **Gobelets**: ou givre de profondeur. Cristaux de neige sans cohésion en forme de pyramide creuse de 5 mm ou plus. Constituent une zone de rupture du manteau neigeux.
- **Langue**: partie terminale d'un glacier.
- **Ligne de pente**: une balle qui descend une pente, marque la ligne de pente (ou ligne de plus grande pente).

- **Main courante**: corde fixée pour servir de rampe.
- **Métamorphose**: processus de transformation du manteau neigeux; on parle de métamorphose destructive, métamorphose constructive, et de métamorphose en gradians.
- **Miner**: déclenchement artificiel d'une avalanche par des explosifs.
- **Moraine**: débris de la montagne charriés par le glacier; sur les côtés (moraines latérales); dessous (moraine de fond); ou devant (moraine frontale).
- **"Peuf"**: la poussière en parlé savoyard; désigne la neige poudreuse.
- **Plaque à vent**: couche de neige compacte, peu élastique, de densité élevée, mal solidarisée avec la sous-couche. Se forme massivement "sous le vent" (sur le versant opposé au vent) et représente le danger n° 1 pour le skieur hors-pistes.
- **Pot**: crevasse en argot montagnard.
- **Purger**: déclencher une avalanche volontairement; purger une pente.
- **Profil stratigraphique**: représentation graphique du manteau neigeux. On trouve en ordonnées la hauteur de neige au-dessus du sol (1 cm de neige = 1 mm) et en abscisses la résistance en Kg. (R 1 Kg. = 1 mm).
- **Rimaye**: ultime crevasse séparant un glacier (qui bouge) de son environnement (qui est fixe).
- **Rive**: côté d'un glacier pris dans le sens orographique du terme; ainsi "rive gauche" veut dire à gauche en descendant.
- **Séracs**: monolithes de glace que l'on rencontre aux points de rupture d'un glacier (ruptures de pente), formant chaos.
- **Sondage de battage**: technique de sondage du manteau neigeux destinée à mesurer l'épaisseur et la densité des couches.
- **Ubac**: versant à l'ombre (exposition nord) d'une vallée.
- **Varosses**: terme savoyard désignant les petits arbustes souvent présents dans les couloirs d'avalanches.

LES BONNES ADRESSES

Pour se renseigner:
- Office de Haute-Montagne: place de l'Eglise - Chamonix Tél. 04 50 53 22 08. Une équipe très compétente au service de tous les conquérants de l'Alpe.
- **Les services des pistes**: ce sont eux les vrais spécialistes de chaque station; n'hésitez pas à leur demander conseil.
- Le drapeau à damier noir et jaune indique qu'il y a risque d'avalanche: on le trouve au départ des remontées mécaniques.
- **Les services météorologiques**:
  - Chamonix-Météo: 08 36 68 02 74. Minitel: 3615 + METEO
  - Répondeur nivo-météorologique:
    (Chablais, Mont-Blanc, Aravis) 08 36 68 10 20. Minitel: 3615 + MTOLY
    Les bulletins font régulièrement référence à l'échelle de risque d'avalanche.

Pour apprendre:
Nous vous conseillons vivement de découvrir le hors-pistes auprès des professionnels compétents: les moniteurs de ski, et les guides (ces derniers sont les seuls à pouvoir exercer leur profession sur les terrains glaciaires).

- Voici quelques adresses:
  - Compagnie des Guides de Chamonix / Ecole de Ski de Chamonix:
    Maison de la Montagne, pl. de l'Eglise, tél. 04 50 53 00 88 / 04 50 53 22 57.
  - Association Internationale des Guides du Mont-Blanc:
    98, rue des Moulins - 74400 Chamonix, tél. 04 50 53 27 05.
  - Ski Sensation, tél. 04 50 53 56 46.
  - Evolution 2, tél. 04 50 55 90 22.
  - Ecole de Ski d'Argentière (et bureau des Guides):
    rue Charlet-Straton, tél. 04 50 54 00 12.
  - Summit: chemin Glacière, Argentière - tél. 04 50 54 05 11.
  - Centres U.C.P.A. d'Argentière, tél. 04 50 54 07 11,
    et de Chamonix, tél. 04 50 53 12 05.
  - Ecole de Ski et Maison des Guides de Vallorcine, tél. 04 50 54 61 67.

Secours: Pelotons de Gendarmerie de Haute Montagne, tél. 04 50 53 16 89.

ECHELLE EUROPEENNE DE RISQUE D'AVALANCHE

à l'intention du public pratiquant la montagne hors des pistes balisées et ouvertes

Indice du risque	Stabilité du manteau neigeux	Probabilité de déclenchement
1. Faible	Le manteau neigeux est bien stabilisé dans la plupart des pentes.	Les déclenchements d'avalanches ne sont possibles que dans de très rares pentes raides (*), surtout par forte surcharge (***). Seules des coulées ou de petites avalanches peuvent se produire spontanément.
2. Limité	Dans quelques (**) pentes suffisamment raides, le manteau neigeux n'est que modérément stabilisé. Ailleurs, il est bien stabilisé.	Déclenchements d'avalanches possibles surtout par forte surcharge (***) et dans quelques pentes dont les caractéristiques sont généralement décrites dans le bulletin. Des départs spontanés d'avalanches de grande ampleur ne sont pas à attendre
3. Marqué	Dans de nombreuses (**) pentes suffisamment raides, le manteau neigeux n'est que modérément à faiblement stabilisé.	Déclenchements d'avalanches possibles parfois même par faible surcharge et dans de nombreuses pentes dont les caractéristiques sont généralement décrites dans le bulletin. Dans certaines situations, quelques départs spontanés d'avalanches de taille moyenne, et parfois assez grosse, sont possibles.
4. Fort	Le manteau neigeux est faiblement stabilisé dans la plupart (**) des pentes suffisamment raides.	Déclenchements d'avalanches possibles même par faible surcharge (***) dans la plupart des pentes suffisamment raides. Dans certaines situations, de nombreux départs spontanés d'avalanches de taille moyenne, et parfois grosse, sont à attendre.
5. Très fort	L'instabilité du manteau neigeux est généralisée.	De nombreuses et grosses avalanches se produisant spontanément sont à attendre y compris en terrain peu raide.

(*)   Pentes particulièrement propices aux avalanches, en raison de leur déclivité, la configuration du terrain, la proximité de la crête...

(**) Les caractéristiques de ces pentes sont généralement précisées dans le bulletin: altitude, exposition, topographie...

(***) Surcharge indicative =
   - **forte**: par exemple, skieurs groupés...
   - **faible**: par exemple, skieur isolé, piéton...

Le terme "déclenchement" concerne les avalanches provoquées par surcharge, notamment par le(s) skieur(s).
Le terme "départ spontané" concerne les avalanches qui se produisent sans action extérieure.

USEFUL ADDRESSES

Information:
- *Office de Haute Montagne:*
  place de l'Eglise - Chamonix, tél: 04 50 53 22 08.
  A very competent team at the service of all mountain users.
- ***Ski Patrol***: *the real specialists of each station. Don't hesitate to ask their advice. The black and yellow chequered flag indicates that there is an avalanche risk. One finds it at the bottom of the lift system.*
- ***Weather Services***:
  - *Chamonix-Meteo: 08 36 68 02 74 - Minitel: 3615 + METEO*
  - *Forecast on an answering machine:*
    (Chablais, Mont-Blanc, Aravis) 08 36 68 10 20. Minitel 3615 + MTOLY.
    The bulletins refer regularly to the level of avalanche risk.

Starting Out:
We sincerely advise you to discover off-piste skiing with a competent professional: a ski instructor or a guide. (In Europe, guides are the only professionals authorised to exercise on glaciated terrain).
- *Here are several addresses:*
  - *Association Internationale des Guides du Mont-Blanc: 98, rue des Moulins Chamonix 74400, tél. 04 50 53 27 05.*
  - *Ski Sensation, tél. 04 50 53 56 46.*
  - *Evolution 2, tél. 04 50 55 90 22.*
  - *Summit: chemin Glacière, Argentière, tél. 04 50 54 05 11.*
  - *Compagnie des Guides de Chamonix / Ecole de Ski de Chamonix: Maison de la Montagne, place de l'Eglise, tél. 04 50 53 00 88 / 04 50 53 22 57.*
  - *Ecole de Ski d'Argentière (and Guides Bureau):*
    rue Charlet-Stratton, tél. 04 50 54 00 12.
  - *U.C.P.A. centres at Argentière, tél. 04 50 54 07 11*
    and at Chamonix, tél. 04 50 53 12 05.
  - *Ecole de Ski et Maison des Guides de Vallorcine, tél. 04 50 54 61 67.*

Mountain rescue: P.G.H.M., tél. 04 50 53 16 89.

EUROPEAN SCALE OF AVALANCHE RISK

for the information of the public using the mountains away from marked, open trails

Risk index	Snowpack stability	Probability of triggering
1. Weak	*The snowpack is well stabilised on most slopes.*	*Triggering of avalanches is only possible on a very few steep slopes (*) especially if heavily overloaded (***). Only small avalanches and snowslides occur spontaneously.*
2. Limited	*On several (**) sufficiently steep slopes, the snowpack is only moderately stabilised. Elsewhere, it is well stabilised.*	*Triggering of avalanches possible, especially if heavily overloaded (***), on some slopes whose characteristics are generally described in the bulletin. Spontaneous avalanches of any size are not to be expected.*
3. Pronounced	*On many (**) sufficiently steep slopes, the snowpack is only moderately to poorly stabilised.*	*Triggering of avalanches possible, sometimes even if slightly overloaded, on many slopes whose characteristics are generally described in the bulletin. In certain situations, some spontaneous medium sized, sometimes fairly large, avalanches are possible.*
4. Strong	*The snowpack is poorly stabilised on most (**) sufficiently steep slopes.*	*Triggering of avalanches possible, even if slightly overloaded (***), on most sufficiently steep slopes. In certain situations, many spontaneous medium size, sometimes large, avalanches are to be expected.*
5. Very strong	*Generalised instability of the snowpack.*	*Numerous large spontaneous avalanches are to be expected, including on terrain that is not very steep.*

(*)   Slopes particulary prone to avalanches, because of their gradient, ground configuration, proximity to a ridge...
(**) The characteristics of these slopes are generally explained in the bulletin: altitude, aspect, topography...
(***) Overloading code =
- **heavy**: for example, grouped skiers...
- **slight**: for example, isolated skier, pedestrian...

The term "triggering" concerns avalanches caused by overloading, in particular by skiers.
The term "spontaneous" concerns avalanches which occur without external action.

LE MATERIEL

Le choix d'un matériel adapté garantit les meilleures conditions de confort et de sécurité. Un sérieux apprentissage théorique et pratique est indispensable afin d'utiliser efficacement les matériels de sécurité (A.R.V.A., corde, crampons) et de navigation (altimètre, boussole, carte, GPS).

▶ **A.R.V.A**: appareil de recherche de victime d'avalanches; indispensable dès que l'on quitte la piste. Veiller au bon fonctionnement de l'appareil avant la descente (piles). A placer sous les vêtements; peut se louer.

▶ **Pelle à neige**: indispensable complément de l'A.R.V.A.; permet de gagner un temps précieux en cas de recherche d'une victime. Une pelle par skieur.

▶ **Sac à dos**: ni trop grand, ni trop petit (30 litres). Une ceinture et une sangle de liaison des bretelles assurent une meilleure tenue sur le dos.

▶ **Carte**: indispensable également; au 1/25000e.

▶ **Boussole**: nécessaire complément de la carte.

▶ **Altimètre**: très utile pour les itinéraires d'envergure.

▶ **Navigateur GPS**: en montagne, le navigateur se montre efficace pour s'orienter sur les zones dégagées (dômes, glaciers). Le positionnement est moins précis sur les versants raides orientés nord.

▶ **Corde**: 30 m de 8, 5 mm. Indispensable sur glacier. Pour des itinéraires peu fréquentés, compter une corde pour deux skieurs.

▶ **Sonde à neige**: indispensable pour accélérer la recherche. Permet d'évaluer à quelle profondeur est ensevelie la victime. Une sonde par skieur.

Voici quelques conseils pour le reste du matériel:

▶ **Les skis**: la nouvelle génération de skis, plus courts et plus larges, facilitent l'apprentissage du ski en toutes neiges. Veillez à ce qu'ils soient bien entretenus: fartage et aiguisage.

▶ **Les fixations**: en neige difficile, resserrez-les afin d'éviter les déclenchements intempestifs dûs à la résistance de la neige.

▶ **Les chaussures**: les mêmes que pour le ski de piste.

▶ **Les bâtons**: il existe des modèles intéressants pouvant se transformer en sonde à avalanche (téléscopiques).

▶ **Le baudrier**: utile dès lors qu'on évolue sur un glacier.

▶ **Les crampons, le piolet**: à prévoir pour certains itinéraires glaciaires.

▶ **Broches à glace**: deux broches afin de confectionner un ancrage en cas de chute en crevasse.

▶ **Anneaux de corde**: 3 anneaux de 5,5 mm pour confectionner un dispositif de sauvetage (nœuds auto-bloquants) et un grand anneau pour faire "pédale".

▶ **Tenue de ski**: chaude et étanche.

▶ **Masque**: très appréciable dans la poudreuse.

▶ **Gants**: très chauds et étanches (surtout si l'on tombe souvent...)

▶ **Lanières**: assurent la liaison ski-chaussures. Pour ne pas perdre ses skis dans la profonde.

▶ **Pharmacie**: au moins une couverture de survie et des pansements compressifs.

En zone glaciaire, chaque skieur devra porter sur son baudrier: 2 broches à glace, 2 systèmes autobloquants (mécanique comme le Ropman, ou des anneaux de cordelettes), un anneau de sangle et 4 mousquetons à vis.

EQUIPMENT

The right choice of equipment offers the best conditions of comfort and security. Don't forget that the avalanche tranceivers, crampons and rope need a certain amount of training to be used efficiently.

▶ **Avalanche Transceiver**: *necessary from the moment one leaves the piste. Check the batteries regularly. To be worn under the clothes; available for hire.*

▶ **Snow Shovel**: *inseparable from the avalanche tranceiver. One gains precious time recovering a victim. Each person in a group should carry one.*

▶ **Back pack**: *neither too big nor too small (around 30 litres). A hip-belt and an elastic liaison between the shoulder straps ensure stability.*

▶ **Map**: *indispensible: 1/25000.*

▶ **Compass**: *goes with map.*

▶ **Altimetre**: *very useful for those wide-ranging descents.*

▶ **GPS navigator**: *an efficient system when terrain is open (glaciers, domes).*

▶ **Rope**: *30 m of 8,5 mm. A must for glaciated terrain. For routes which don't see much traffic, you should carry one rope for two people.*

▶ **Avalanche probe**: *for the fast and safe pin-point search of avalanche victim. Each person in a group should carry one.*

Some advice for the remainder of the equipment.

▶ **Skis**: *the latest generation of skis, shorter and wider than their predecessors, make learning how to ski in deep snow much easier. Make sure they are well maintained - waxed and sharpened.*

▶ **Bindings**: *in difficult snow, tighten them to avoid pre-release due to the snow's resistance.*

▶ **Boots**: *keep your usual boots (if you're happy with them).*

▶ **Poles**: *there exist telescopic models which transform into avalanche probes.*

▶ **Harness**: *good idea when on a glacier.*

Off-piste skiing on glaciers : each person should carry on their harness: 2 ice screws, 2 rope ascenders (either mechanical camming units like the Ropeman, or loops of rope), a foot-sling and 4 locking carabiners.

Photo: *Tim BARNETT*

L'ENNEMI NUMERO 1: L'AVALANCHE
COMMENT DETERMINER LE RISQUE?

Association Nationale pour l'Etude de la Neige et des Avalanches - (**ANENA**)
15, rue Ernest Calvat -38000 GRENOBLE
Tél. 04 76 51 39 39

Beaucoup de facteurs interviennent dans la détermination des conditions avalancheuses. Les principaux sont:

1. Le terrain - Le danger d'avalanches croît avec la pente du terrain: au-delà de 25° environ par rapport à l'horizontale, tout versant enneigé peut être instable: certaines "plaques" formées par le vent peuvent se déclencher en avalanches pour des inclinaisons encore plus faibles. Des terrains de très faible pente, voire horizontaux, peuvent être balayés par des avalanches venues des régions supérieures. Des bas de versant peuvent être menacés par des avalanches venues s'écraser à partir du versant d'en face.

Le danger d'avalanches dépend aussi de la nature du terrain, de son profil, de son exposition au soleil ou au vent.

2. La neige fraîche - Une chute de neige fraîche provoque dans les jours qui suivent, et selon son importance, un accroissement du danger.

Si, dans les dernières 24 heures, il est tombé:

20 à 30 cm de neige	: augmentation appréciable du danger.
30 à 50 cm	: danger déjà sérieux dans les parties raides des parcours skiables.
50 à 100 cm	: danger sensible menaçant déjà les troncons exposés des voies de communication.
au-delà de 100 cm	: danger généralisé et fréquemment étendu aux habitations situées dans des zones exposées.

3. La structure du manteau neigeux - Des couches intérieures fragiles peuvent rendre la couverture de neige moins stable. Une surcharge temporaire peut alors provoquer la rupture des ancrages.

4. Le vent

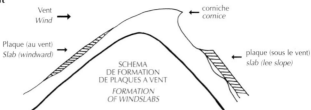

Vent
Wind

corniche
cornice

Plaque (au vent)
Slab (windward)

plaque (sous le vent)
slab (lee slope)

SCHEMA
DE FORMATION
DE PLAQUES A VENT

*FORMATION
OF WINDSLABS*

Il transporte la neige et l'accumule dans les endroits abrités sous forme de **"plaques"** particulièrement dangereuses.

Un **vent chaud** (fœhn) accroît le plus souvent le risque (surtout si la durée du phènoméne est prolongée).

5. La température

a) Pour la neige froide et sèche. Par basse température, au-dessous de 0° C, le danger d'avalanches de **"poudreuse"** peut persister pendant plusieurs jours après la fin de la chute.

b) Une élévation de température (notamment au-dessus de 0° C) augmente le risque immédiat d'avalanches, mais provoque aussi le tassement de la neige (consolidation).

c) L'alternance de dégel diurne et de regel nocturne provoque la formation des **croûtes** superficielles; lorsque cette croûte est suffisamment épaisse, il n'y a pratiquement plus de danger, même si la couche superficielle se met à fondre sur quelques centimètres d'épaisseur.

d) Pour les **neiges de printemps**, détrempées par la fonte due à l'ensoleillement, ou par la pluie, le risque croît avec la déclivité et avec l'épaisseur de la couche détrempée.

e) Les **plaques** formées par le vent doivent être considérées comme dangereuses à toute température.

D'une façon générale, **neige fraîche, vent et hausse de température** sont des facteurs déterminants capables de provoquer une situation dangereuse sur une pente qui a pu, pendant une période prolongée, présenter un caractère de sécurité.

ENEMY NUMBER 1: AVALANCHES
HOW TO DETERMINE THE RISK?

Many factors determine avalanche conditions. The most influential are:

1. **The terrain** - *The avalanche danger increases with the gradient of the slope: above 25°, every snowy aspect can be unstable: certain "slabs" formed by the wind (windslab) may avalanche towards more stable ground. Gentle slopes, and even flat ground may be swept by avalanches occuring higher up. The runout zone may include in some cases the lower opposite mountainside. The avalanche danger depends also on the nature of the terrain, of it's profile, exposition to the sun or to the wind.*

2. **Fresh snow** - *A fresh snow fall, according to the amount fallen, provokes, in the days which follow, an increase in danger. If, in the last 24 hours there has fallen:*

   20 - 30 cm of snow : appreciable augmentation of danger
   30 - 50 cm   : already serious danger concerning most ski terrain
   50 - 100 cm   : real danger threatening communication lines where exposed.
   above 100 cm   : general danger frequently extending to habitations situated in exposed zones.

3. **The snow-pack structure** - *Fragile interior layers can render the snow-cover less stable. A sudden increase in weight, may then cause a rupture.*

4. **The wind** - *Transports the snow and loads it in sheltered place in the form of particularly dangerous "windslabs". A warm wind (foehn) often increases the risk, particularly if the situation is prolonged.*

5. **Temperature** -
   a) Cold, dry snow. At low temperatures, below 0° C, the danger of "powder" avalanches can persist several days after a snow - fall.

b) A rise in temperature (notably above 0°C) increases the immediate avalanche risk, but also settles the snow, (consolidation or binding).

c) Continued melting and freezing forms superficial crusts. If this crust is sufficiently thick, the danger is practically eliminated, even if the upper crust starts to melt over a depth of several centimetres.

d) For spring snow, waterlogged due to the sun or rain, the risk augments with an increase in slope and with the thickness of the waterlogged layer.

e) Slabs formed by the wind (windslab) must be considered as dangerous at any temperature.

Generally speaking, fresh snow, wind and a rise in temperature are the determining factors capable of provoking a dangerous situation on a slope which has seemed safe for a prolonged period leading up to the change in conditions.

LE SKI SUR GLACIER

Dès qu'on aborde la haute montagne, les compétences d'alpinisme doivent compléter les qualités de skieur. Le concours d'un guide professionnel est, à nos yeux, la solution la plus sûre pour débuter l'apprentissage d'un milieu aussi hostile. Le glacier ajoute des dangers supplémentaires aux risques d'avalanches: les crevasses, les dévissages sur la glace, et les chutes de séracs.

- Les crevasses:

L'ennemi numéro 1. Si les plus grosses sont identifiables à condition de maîtriser sa vitesse (on a secouru en même temps jusqu'à trois personnes tombées dans la même crevasse!); la plupart du temps, elles sont recouvertes par la neige, formant des ponts qui peuvent céder sous le poids des skieurs.

- Dévissage sur glace:

Les zones raides des glaciers, langues terminales, dômes, sont à aborder avec prudence. Une simple pellicule de neige peut en effet recouvrir la glace vive.

- Les séracs:

Les glaciers bougent et des masses énormes de glace peuvent être déséquilibrées à tous moments.

Conseils:

- s'assurer de l'enneigement du glacier avant de descendre (éviter les débuts d'hiver);
- skier tôt le matin, quand le froid soude les ponts de neige;
- rester maître de sa vitesse;
- ne jamais déchausser les skis, même pour une urgence;
- sonder du bâton les ponts suspects - s'encorder si nécessaire;
- franchir les ponts de neige avec une certaine vitesse pour ne pas s'arrêter dessus.

GLACIER SKIING

When one ventures into high mountains, the qualities of an alpinist must complement the qualities of a skier. The services of a professional Guide is, in our eyes, the surest way to ease one 's debut in this hostile environment. Glaciers add other dangers to the avalanche risk: crevasses, sliding falls on ice and serac fall.

- The crevasses:
Enemy number one. The biggest are usually avoidable on condition that one masters his speed (there is a case where 3 people fell into the same hole successively). Often covered by the snow, these "snow-bridges" can break under the weight of a skier.

- Slipping:
The steep zones of a glacier must be treated with respect. Glacier terminals and domes may be covered simply with a dusting of fresh snow hiding the "bullet-proof" ice underneath.

- The Seracs:
The glaciers move and these towers of ice may topple at any time. Esthetic but picnic somewhere else!

Advice:
- make sure the snow-cover of a glacier is sufficient **before** starting out. Avoid early winter and late spring;
- ski early in the morning, when the snow-bridges are frozen;
- stay in **control**;
- never take off your skis, even for a toilet stop!
- probe for suspect crevasses with your poles. Rope up if necessary;
- cross snow-bridges with a bit of speed so as not to stop on them.

CONDUITE D'UNE DESCENTE

Contrairement au ski de piste, où chacun peut évoluer où bon lui semble grâce au balisage et à la signalisation du moindre danger, la sécurité en hors-pistes dépend en grande partie de l'attitude collective du groupe: organisation, discipline, choix de la trace.

- Organisation du groupe:
- skier par petit groupe de 3 à 6 personnes de niveau homogène. Trois personnes permettent de faire face à un accident (alerte et recherche d'une victime);
- les skieurs les plus expérimentés ouvrent et ferment la marche;
- répartir le matériel de façon judicieuse. Les derniers de la caravane portent le matériel de secours (pelle, cordes..);
- prévoir de fréquents arrêts-regroupements afin de ne jamais laisser un skieur à la traîne.

- Discipline du groupe:
- le skieur de tête recherche l'itinéraire, identifie les dangers, donne des consignes de sécurité au reste du groupe (distance d'espacement, respect de la trace, etc...);
- le groupe doit se regrouper en amont du skieur de pointe. En cas d'arrêt d'urgence (crevasse) il est préférable de ne pas le dépasser...

- Faire la trace:
L'itinéraire le plus sûr n'est pas toujours le plus court ni le plus logique. D'un endroit à l'autre les risques ne seront pas les mêmes. Quelques principes doivent guider vos choix:
- contre-pente, rupture de pente, où se forment plaques à vent et accumulations, doivent être évitées;
- les pentes irrégulières sont plus sûres que les pentes uniformes;
- éviter les longues traversées à flanc de pente;
- préférer les croupes neigeuses; les pentes parsemées d'ilots rocheux;
- si une traversée est obligatoire, la tenter le plus haut possible.

Conseils:
dans les zones estimées dangereuses, ne s'engager qu'un à un, d'abri en abri (arbre, rocher...); on observe le skieur en action. On ôte: les dragonnes des bâtons et une bretelle du sac à dos. On s'habille chaudement.

CONDUCTING A DESCENT

Contrary to piste skiing where the slightest danger is marked, off-piste safety depends mostly on the collective attitude of the group: organisation, discipline, route chosen.

- **Group organisation**:
  - ski in a small group of 3-6 people with the same standard. Three people is the minimum in case of accident (alert, and/or search);
  - the most experienced skiers ski first and last;
  - distribute the equipment sensibly. Those carrying the rope, shovel etc. ski last;
  - regroup systematically when skiing.

- **Group discipline**:
  - the lead skier route-finds, identifying the dangers, giving advice to the rest of the group (spacing, where to ski etc..),
  - the group must stop above the lead skier in case of urgency (crevasse), better to remain above the danger.

- **Route-finding**:
  The surest way is not always the shortest nor the most logical. From one place to another the risks are never the same. Some advice:
  - the sides of gullies and convex roils must be avoided as they are subject to windslab loading;
  - irregular slopes are safer than big uniform slopes;
  - avoid long traverses across the slope;
  - give preference to snowy rumps, rolls and slopes with scattered rock "islands";
  - if a traverse is unavoidable, traverse as high as possible.

Important:
in a dangerous area, progress one by one and from shelter to shelter (tree, rock..). Observe the skier in action. Undo: ski straps, wriststrap and one shoulder-strap of your backpack. Dress warmly.

QUE FAIRE EN CAS D'ACCIDENT?

On peut distinguer **3** types d'accidents dans la pratique du hors-pistes. Les chutes en crevasse, les ensevelissements par avalanche, et les traumatismes dûs à une mauvaise chute. Toutefois, avant de voir chacun de ces cas, voici un ensemble de conseils valables pour toutes les situations.

Tout d'abord la règle que l'on apprend dans les stages de secourisme pour ordonner son action en cas d'accident est aussi valable en montagne, à savoir; PROTEGER, ALERTER, SECOURIR.

- PROTEGER:

C'est à dire mettre la victime hors de nouveaux dangers; à l'abri d'une éventuelle coulée, dans un endroit où elle ne risque pas de dévisser; la couvrir chaudement; on marquera sa position par des skis plantés croisés 6 ou 7 mètres en amont, pour éviter que d'autre skieurs puissent la percuter.

- ALERTER:

Si des professionnels (guides, moniteurs) sont à proximité, alertez-les: ils ont probablement une radio qui leur permettra de prévenir aussitôt les gendarmes-secouristes. Sinon, localisez parfaitement l'endroit où vous êtes, rassurez la victime et rejoignez la remontée mécanique la plus proche, où l'employé donnera l'alerte; fournissez-lui un maximun de renseignements, notamment sur la nature du traumatisme. Surtout, en prévenant les secours, ne confondez pas vitesse et précipitation. Il n'est malheureusement pas rare qu'un accident survienne à une personne tentant de donner l'alerte. En tout état de cause le fil conducteur de votre action doit être de ne pas aggraver la situation par une action désespérée, mais plutôt d'agir avec logique et froideur, même si cela, bien évidemment, n'est pas facile à réaliser sous le coup de l'émotion. S'il n'y a pas de remontées mécaniques joignables, gagner le point le plus proche où vous pourrez téléphoner: contactez le Peloton de Gendarmerie en Haute Montagne, P.G.H.M., au 04.50.53.16.89.

- SECOURIR:

On verra plus loin les particularités de chaque situation. En ce qui concerne l'intervention des secouristes, il est probable qu'elle s'effectuera en hélicoptère. Voici, sur ce point, les conseils d'usage à respecter scrupuleusement:
- la zone où l'hélicoptère va intervenir doit être la plus plate possible - si c'est envisageable déplacer la victime - et préférer une proéminence à un creux;

- calez tout ce qui peut s'envoler et réunissez les skis à plat (sauf ceux qui, bien en amont, délimitent la zone d'intervention);
- utilisez les signes conventionnels de demande de secours (voir schéma);
- placez-vous bien en vue, vent dans le dos, les bras en V (si vous ne parvenez pas à être localisé, agitez un anorak);
- quand l'hélicoptère s'approchera, posez un genou à terre, baissez les bras, mais ne partez surtout pas: vous êtes son seul point de repère à cause de la neige qui vole et supprime toute visibilité;
- dès lors, faites-leur absolument confiance: ce sont des spécialistes horspair. Sachez toutefois qu'un hélicoptère s'aborde toujours par l'avant de façon à être dans le champ visuel du pilote, et que l'on y rentre toujours par son côté gauche.

- Cas d'une chute en crevasse:

Si vous êtes bon alpiniste, pas seul, correctement équipé et aguerri aux manœuvres de cordes, effectuez un mouflage de surface. Sinon rassurez, autant que faire se peut, la victime: il est possible que vous ne l'entendiez pas mais qu'elle vous entende. Ne vous approchez surtout pas du bord, qui pourrait s'effondrer. Essayez d'alerter d'autres skieurs. Si vous êtes seul, localisez bien le lieu de l'accident: marquez la crevasse d'affaires solidement amarrées et bien visibles. Et partez, avec un maximum de prudence, prévenir les secours.

- Cas d'accident par avalanche: (document A.N.E.N.A.)

A. Conduite à tenir par la personne surprise par l'avalanche:

1. Tenter la fuite latérale.
2. Se débarrasser des bâtons et du sac.
3. Fermer la bouche et protéger les voies respiratoires pour éviter à tout prix de remplir ses poumons de neige.
4. Essayer de se cramponner à tout obstacle pour éviter d'être emporté.
5. Essayer de se maintenir à la surface.
6. Ne pas s'essouffler en criant. Pour tenter de se faire entendre: émettre des sons brefs et aigus. L'idéal serait un sifflet.
7. Faire le maximum d'efforts pour se dégager au moment où l'on sent que l'avalanche va s'arrêter; au moment de l'arrêt, si l'ensevelissement est total, s'efforcer de créer une poche en exécutant une détente énergique, puis ne plus bouger pour économiser l'air.

B. Conduite à tenir par les témoins:

1. Marquer l'endroit où le disparu a été vu pour la dernière fois.
2. Examen de toute la surface de l'avalanche. S'il n'y a qu'un rescapé, aller chercher du secours, si aucun signe de localisation n'est perçu.
3. S'il y a plusieurs rescapés:
   - donner l'alerte au poste de secours le plus proche avec toutes précisions utiles (1 ou 2 personnes).
   - maintenir ou installer le poste d'alerte pour le cas où de nouvelles coulées seraient à craindre.
   - mettre les appareils émetteurs-récepteurs sur "réception".
4. Essayer de localiser les disparus
   - probablement dans la direction de l'avalanche, au-dessous du point de disparition.
   - de préférence dans les replats, en amont des obstacles.
   - sur les abords du cône d'accumulation (notamment dans le cas où l'avalanche s'est déclenchée au-dessus des sinistrés).
5. Tenter de découvrir des objets (vêtements, cordelette, bâton) à la surface de la neige, ou un membre émergeant de l'avalanche. Ecouter. Marquer les endroits où l'on découvre quelque chose et les fouiller immédiatement avec les bâtons (enlever les poignées et si possible les rondelles) ou avec les talons des skis, si, comme c'est le cas en général, on ne dispose pas de sondes.
6. Rechercher avec les ARVA suivant les instructions fournies par le fabricant. Rappelons qu'il est essentiel d'effectuer des manœuvres d'entraînement pour se familiariser avec le maniement de ces appareils.
7. Procéder si les victimes ne sont pas munies d'un ARVA,
   - d'abord à un sondage sommaire, par coups de sonde aux endroits présumés favorables.
   - puis à un sondage large et méthodique (un coup de sonde entre les pieds, écarts 70 à 75 cm, profondeur optimale 2 m).
   - enfin à un sondage serré (3 coups de sondes à chaque station, écarts de 25 à 30 cm, profondeur optimale 3 m).

Rappelons qu'il ne faut ni fumer, ni uriner sur l'avalanche (au cas où les chiens interviendraient). **LA RAPIDITE DE LA LOCALISATION ET DES SECOURS SONT LES FACTEURS DU SUCCES.**

C. Conduite à tenir vis à vis de la victime:

1. Dans l'ordre
   - libérer complètement la tête,
   - débarrasser la bouche et le nez de la neige et de l'eau,
   - dégager le corps et, si les circonstances l'exigent, transporter la victime en lieu sûr.

2. Si la victime **n'a pas perdu connaissance:**
   - la réchauffer (couvertures, boissons chaudes),
   - en cas de blessures, lui donner les premiers soins,
   - en cas de vomissements, la coucher sur le ventre,
   - la transporter rapidement à l'abri ou dans la vallée.

3. Si la victime est **sans connaissance** mais **respire encore:**
   - la mettre en **position latérale de sécurité** pour éviter la noyade dans les liquides de régurgitation,
   - procéder comme ci-dessus mais pas de boisson.

4. Si la victime **ne donne plus signe de vie** (arrêt de respiration, voire arrêt du pouls):
   - libérer complètement les voies respiratoires,
   - pratiquer la **respiration artificielle** (bouche à bouche),
   - pratiquer le **massage cardiaque, externe**,
   - protéger la victime du froid comme indiqué ci-dessus. Pas de boisson,
   - continuer sans relâche, la respiration artificielle associée au massage cardiaque externe, jusqu'à résultat heureux ou jusqu'à l'arrivée du médecin ou jusqu'à apparition des signes certains de la mort (réflexe des paupières, rigidité cadavérique),
   - ne déplacer la victime inanimée que si la respiration artificielle peut être assurée sans interruption pendant le transport, ainsi que le massage cardiaque externe.

- **Cas de traumatisme dû à une chute**: Si vous pouvez demeurer sur place tandis qu'une autre personne est partie alerter les secours, il vous est à présent possible d'apporter les premiers soins à la victime. Là encore, ne tentez pas l'impossible, mais contentez-vous des actes dont vous êtes **absolument sûr**; et surtout éviter de déplacer votre compagnon s'il y a risque de traumatisme de la colonne vertébrale.

ALERTER LES SECOURS EST UN ACTE GRAVE. SEUL UN ACCIDENT AUQUEL, A' L'EVIDENCE, ON NE PEUT FAIRE FACE SEUL JUSTIFIE LA MISE-EN-OEUVRE DE CE GENRE D'OPERATION, SOUVENT PERILLEUSE.

SIGNAUX DE DÉTRESSE

Se tenir debout,
bras levés, immobile

Carré de tissu rouge
d'un mètre de côté
avec un cercle blanc

Fusée rouge de détresse,
très efficace, surtout la
nuit. En vente dans les
magasins de sport
spécialisés

**NOUS DEMANDONS
DU
SECOURS**

Se tenir debout, un seul
bras levé, immobile

**NOUS N'AVONS
BESOIN
DE RIEN**

Numéro de téléphone du Peloton de Gendarmerie
de haute montagne: **04.50.53.16.89**

WHAT TO DO IN CASE OF ACCIDENT?

*One can distinguish **3** types of accidents relating to off-piste skiing. Falls into crevasses; avalanche injuries, and traumatisms due to a bad sliding fall. Before looking separately at each case; here is some valuable advice for all situations. First of all the golden rule that one learns in first-aid courses applies also in the mountains: ie. PROTECT, ALERT, RESCUE.*

- PROTECT:
  That's to say keep the victim out of new danger; sheltered from a new avalanche, in a place where the victim doesn't risk slipping; cover the victim warmly; mark the victim is position by planting crossed skis 6-7 metres above, to avoid collisions.

- ALERT:
  Signal the guides and ski-instructors if they are close by; probably someone has a radio. If not, locate exactly the place where you are, reassure the victim then go for the nearest help. Once help is found, give a maximum of information, above all on the nature of the injury.
  On alerting the rescue services, don't rush. Unfortunately it is not rare that an accident arrives to the person giving the alert. Remain calm, think coldly and logically, which is not always easy in an emotional situation. If there are no lifts nearby, on having reached a telephone contact the mountain police, the P.G.H.M.; 04.50.53.16.89.

- RESCUE:
  We will discuss further the particularities of different situations.
  Concerning the rescuers, they will probably arrive by helicopter.
  Some advice to respect scrupulously:
  - the zone where the helicopter lands must be as flat as possible. If it is possible to move the victim choose a prominant point instead of a hollow;
  - fix everything which could fly away and lay the skis down (except those marking the accident zone).
  - use conventional rescue signs (see distress signals);
  - remain well in sight, back to the wind, the arms in a V (if you still haven't been found, wave an anorak);

- when the helicopter arrives, get down on one knee, lower your arms but don't move an inch. You are the pilot's only reference point because of the flying snow;
- from this point on, have confidence in the pilot. He knows what he's doing. Remember that a helicopter is approached always from the front, remaining in view of the pilot and that one enters always on the left side of the helicopter.

- **Fall into Crevasse**:

If you are a good alpinist, correctly equipped and familiar with rope manœuvres, make a Z-pulley and winch the victim to the surface.

If not, reassure the victim as best you can. Maybe you can't hear him but he can hear you. Don't approach too close to the crevasse edge, which might collapse.

Try alerting other skiers. If you are alone, locate exactly the accident site: mark the hole with something well anchored and easily visible. Go for help, being extremely cautious on the way.

- **Avalanche**:

A. If caught in an avalanche:
1. Try escaping laterally.
2. Get rid of poles and backpack.
3. Keep mouth closed and protect the air passages from snow entering the lungs. N.B. Important.
4. Try to grasp anything to help you from being carried down.
5. Try to stay on the surface.
6. Don't tire yourself out by shouting; emit short, sharp sounds. A whistle is best.
7. Make a big effort to free yourself when you feel the avalanche is about to stop; if buried totally try to create an air pocket by moving energetically, and also to compensate the snow's crushing effect.

B. What to do if you witness an avalanche:
1. **Mark the place** where the victim was last seen.
2. Examine the debris rapidly, over it's entire surface. Go for help if no sign is found.
3. If there are survivors on the surface:
   - **give the alert** at the nearest post possible, relaying precisely all information.

    - maintain or install a **look-out** if new avalanches are possible.

    - turn avalanche tranceivers on to recieve.

4. Try **to locate the victims**.

    - probably in the direction of the avalanche below where they last were seen.

    - likely to be in the levelling off above a natural obstacle.

    - On the sides of the debris cone (especially when the avalanche triggered itself off above the victims).

5. **Look for objects** (clothes, poles, etc.) on the snow's surface, or a projecting limb. Listen. Mark the places where you find something and search immediately with your poles (Take off the wrist-grips and if possible the baskets) or with the tails of your skis, if, as in most cases one does not have probes at his disposal.

6. Search with the avalanche tranceivers, following the maker's instructions. Remember that training is **necessary** to use these devices correctly, and quickly.

7. If the victims are not equipped with avalanche tranceivers.

    - Start a quick probe, in likely places.

    - If unsuccessful commence a wide, methodic probe, (probe between the feet every 70 - 75 cm, optimal depth 2 metres).

    - Then a thorough probe, 25-30 cm a part, depth 3 m.

N.B. One must not smoke or urinate on the avalanche (in case avalanche dogs intervene). THE SPEED OF THE LOCATION AND RESCUE OF THE VICTIMS IS THE KEY TO SUCCESS.

C. When victim is found:

1. In this order:

    - free the head completely.

    - empty the mouth and nose of snow and water

    - free the body and if circumstances dictate, move the victim to a safer place.

2. If the victim is conscious.

    - rewarm him/her (sleeping bag, hot drinks)

    - if injured, give first-aid

    - if vomiting, place victim on his/her stomach.

- transport victim rapidly to shelter or to hospital.

3. If the victim is unconscious:
   - put him/her in recovery position to avoid drowning in vomit (on side, head down).
   - procede as above but no drinks.

4. If the victim gives no vital signs (breathing stopped, no pulse):
   - free completely the air passages
   - give artificial respiration (mouth to mouth, mouth to nose)
   - give external cardiac massage
   - protect the victim from the cold as indicated above. No drinks
   - continue without stopping, the artificial respiration and cardiac massage until a happy result or until the arrival of a doctor or until signs of death are certain (rigid eyelids, rigor mortis)
   - move the inanimate victim only if artificial respiration and cardiac massage can be continued without interruption during the transportation.

- **Traumatism due to a fall**:

   If you must stay while someone else alerts the rescue services, it is up to you to give the necessary first-aid to the victim. Here again, don't try the impossible but make the injured person as comfortable as possible. Be absolutely sure of what you're doing.

   Above all, avoid moving the victim, if there is a risk of injury to the spine. REASSURE THE VICTIM.

ALERTING THE RESCUE SERVICES IS A SERIOUS ACT. ONLY AN ACCIDENT WHERE YOU ARE HELPLESS BY YOURSELF TO DO WHAT IS NECESSARY JUSTIFIES A RESCUE OPERATION, OFTEN PERILOUS FOR THE PERSONNEL.

DISTRESS SIGNALS

Stand up straight,
arms lifted, motionless

Red cloth, one metre
square, with a white circle

Red distress rocket,
very efficient, especially
at night. On sale in
specialised sports shops

**WE
NEED
RESCUING**

Stand up straight,
one arm lifted,
motionless

**WE DON'T
NEED
ANYTHING**

Mountain rescue - P.G.H.M.
Tel.: **04.50.53.16.89**

UTILISATION DES DESCRIPTIONS D'ITINERAIRE

Trois sources d'information doivent guider votre choix d'itinéraire:
- les textes, qui décrivent le cheminement
- les photos (ou dessins): les tracés donnent une idée de la ligne générale, qui peut notablement évoluer en fonction des conditions
- une carte au 1/25000

Deux instruments pourront compléter ces informations:
- la boussole, nécessaire lorsque le texte fourni des repères de direction
- l'altimètre, conseillé pour les descentes de grande envergure; il vous aidera, associé à la carte, à savoir si vous êtes sur le bon chemin.

Nous n'avons que rarement donné des horaires, ceux-ci étant complètement dépendants de votre niveau technique, et des conditions de neige.

Difficulté: nous avons conservé les termes utilisés en alpinisme. Ça donne:

- **Facile (F)**   : pentes douces et larges.
- **Peu difficile (P.D.)**   : pentes un peu plus raides, avec d'éventuels passages étroits.
- **Assez difficile (A.D.)**   : pentes à 20°/25°, pouvant être soutenues.
- **Difficile (D)**   : pentes sérieuses, 30°/35°, où le risque de dévissage existe réellement.
- **Très difficile (T.D.)**   : ski de pentes raides, 40°/45°, nécessitant une bonne maîtrise des techniques spécifiques. Le risque de dévissage est permanent et lourd de conséquences.
- **Extrêmement difficile (E.D.)** : domaine du ski extrême, 45° et au-delà. Réservé aux spécialistes.

Nous avons également donné une estimation sur l'engagement de la descente:

- **Peu engagée**   : à proximité immédiate des pistes.
- **Assez engagée** : déjà à l'écart des pistes, bien que visible de celles-ci et se terminant sur celles-ci.
- **Engagée**   : il y a peu de chances que l'on soit vu en cas d'accident; de plus alerter les secours prendra un certain temps.
- **Très engagée** : "perdus" en haute montagne, les skieurs devront démontrer une autonomie totale dans toutes les situations.

Enfin ces informations sont complétées par des remarques sur la complexité du cheminement et la nature des dangers rencontrés.

USING THE ROUTE DESCRIPTIONS

Three information sources will influence your choice of a route:
  - the texts, which describe the route.
  - the photos (or designs): the lines give an idea of the general direction, which may have changed according to the conditions.
  - a map to the scale of: 1/25000.

Two instruments can help out:
  - the compass, necessary when the text gives bearings to follow
  - the altimetre, handy to have for the big descents; along with the map, it will help you locate your exact position. We have rarely given times, these being completely dependant on your skiing standard and the snow conditions.

Difficulty: we have used the terms used in alpinism; as follows:
  - **Easy**   : wide gentle slopes.
  - **Little difficult** : slopes a little steeper, with narrow passages.
  - **Quite difficult**   : slopes at 20°/25°, may be sustained.
  - **Difficult**   : serious gradient 30°/35° where a real risk of slipping exists.
  - **Very difficult**   : steep skiing 40°/45°, requiring very good, and some-times specific technique. The risk of falling is perma-nent and with heavy consequences.
  - **Extremely difficult** : extreme skiing terrain, above 45°. Reserved for the specialists of the game.

We have also given an estimation of the commitment of the descent:
  - **Not serious**   : close to the pistes.
  - **Quite serious** : far from the marked runs but visible from them and finishing on the piste.
  - **Serious**   : little chance of being seen in case of an accident, what's more, alerting the rescue services will take a certain amount of time.
  - **Very serious**   : isolated in the high mountains, skiers must be com-pletely autonomous in every situation.

These route descriptions are complemented by remarks on the difficulty of the route-finding and the nature of the dangers likely to be met with.

2ème partie

LE PLUS BEAU DOMAINE DU MONDE ...

Part two

THE FINEST SKI TERRAIN IN THE WORLD

LES SITES / *THE AREAS*

- 1. Le Brévent
- 2. La Flégère
- 3. Balme
- 4. Les Grands Montets
- 5. L'Aiguille du Midi
- 6. Toule
- 7. Les Houches

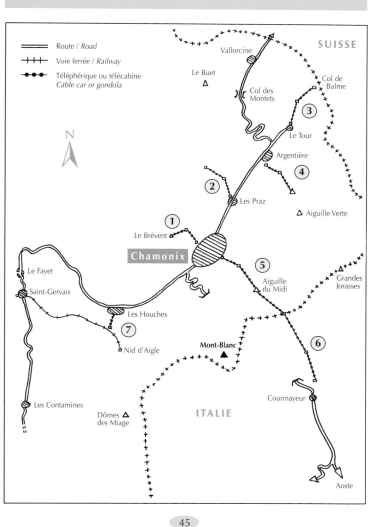

══════	Route / *Road*
┼┼┼┼	Voie ferrée / *Railway*
●─●─●	Téléphérique ou télécabine *Cable car or gondola*

N

SUISSE

Vallorcine

Le Buet
Δ

Col des
Montets

Col de
Balme

③

Le Tour

Argentière

④

②

Les Praz

Δ Aiguille Verte

①

Le Brévent Δ

Chamonix

⑤

Aiguille
du Midi

Grandes
Jorasses

Le Fayet

Saint-Gervais

Les Houches

⑦

Nid d'Aigle

Mont-Blanc ▲

⑥

Courmayeur

Les Containes

Dômes Δ
des Miage

ITALIE

Aoste

LE BRÉVENT

S'il est une remontée qui a contribué à donner à Chamonix la réputation d'une station de ski déconseillée aux âmes sensibles, c'est bien le Brévent. Cet audacieux téléphérique, construit dès 1932, dessert davantage de vertigineux couloirs cernés de murailles rocheuses que les douces prairies traditionnellement associées à la pratique du ski. Et c'était une gageure que d'envisager une station dans un endroit pareil!

Mais le pari est tenu, et, avec les secteurs des Vioz et Cornu, le Brévent possède aujourd'hui un éventail de pistes pour tous les niveaux. Du temps jadis demeure la célèbre piste "Charles Bozon", une noire foncée qui a ému plus d'un skieur émérite.

Côté hors-pistes, nous sommes ici au royaume du ski sauvage: sauvage par l'isolement, l'austérité et l'audace des itinéraires; ceux-ci sont pour la plupart engagés et techniquement très sérieux. En quelques virages on se retrouve dans une haute-montagne sans concession, où l'on doit imaginer un passage au milieu des tours de gneiss, des couloirs étroits, des larges pentes aux lignes fuyantes. Pile en face du Mont-Blanc, des traces d'aventure pour les purs et durs.

If there is one lift which has given Chamonix the reputation of not being a resort for timid souls, it's well and truly the Brévent. This audacious cable-car, built in 1932, serves steep, rock-lined couloirs along with the soft prairies traditionally associated with the practice of skiing. And what an undertaking it was!

But the engineers obviously did their sums correctly, and with the Vioz and Cornu sectors, the Brévent possesses today an inventory of pistes for all skiers - including the infamous "Charles Bozon", a black diamond run which always demands respect.

Concerning the off-piste, here we are in the kingdom of "wild" skiing. Wild by the isolation, the austerity and the audacity of the itineraries; these are for the most part serious and technically demanding. In a few turns one finds oneself in mountain terrain, without concession, searching for a passage amongst towers of gneiss, through narrow couloirs, or down wide but convex slopes. Directly opposite the Mont-Blanc, some adventurous lines for the hard-core await.

Grands couloirs ... / *The main couloirs* ... - photo: *Tim BARNETT*

INFOS

Téléphone : 04 50 53 13 18

Situation : juste au-dessus de Chamonix, sur le versant sud.

Enneigement : exposition sud ne garantissant pas toujours un bon enneigement jusqu'à Chamonix. Le haut est en général bien enneigé. Dès février, la neige est souvent dure le matin, pour se transformer rapidement avec le soleil.

Conditions climatiques : station d'altitude bien ensoleillée.

Cadre : exceptionnel; face au Mont-Blanc.

Accès : du centre de Chamonix, remonter la "Mollard", derrière l'église, jusqu'au départ de la télécabine de Planpraz (500 m). Grand parking.

Restauration : restaurant, self-service et salle hors-sacs à Planpraz, à l'arrivée de la télécabine. Terrasse. Tél.: 04 50 53 05 42; restaurant à "Altitude 2000", au sommet du petit télésiège du même nom. Grande terrasse. Tél.: 04 50 53 15 58.

Liaison : téléphérique rejoignant la Flégère depuis la combe de la Charlanon. Du cœur de Chamonix on peut rejoindre le départ de la télécabine de Planpraz par le téléski du Savoy (si l'enneigement le permet).

Secours : postes de secours à Planpraz et au départ du télésiège du Col Cornu. Possibilité d'alerte en bas de chaque remontée mécanique. En hors-piste, le secours est assuré par le Peloton de Gendarmerie de Haute-Montagne.

INFORMATION

Telephone : 04 50 53 13 18.

Situation : just above Chamonix, on the south side.

Snow : the south-facing slopes don't always guarantee a good base just to Chamonix. Up top there is generally a good cover. From february onwards the snow is often hard in the morning, then transforms rapidly with the sun.

Climatic conditions : station at altitude, very sunny.

Setting : exceptional; straight across from Mont-Blanc.

Access : from Chamonix centre, up the hill behind the church to the tele-cabine "Planpraz" (500 m). Big parking area.

Food : restaurant, self-service and pic-nic room at Planpraz (mid station). Terrace. Tel.: 04 50 53 05 42. Restaurant "Altitude 2000" at the summit of the small chairlift of the same name. Huge terrace. Tel.: 04 50 53 15 58.

Links : with la Flégère; cable-car from the Charlanon piste. From the heart of Chamonix one can reach the Planpraz telecabine by the Savoy T-bar (snow permitting).

Rescue : rescue post at Planpraz and at the start of the Col Cornu chairlift. Alert can be given at the bottom of each lift. Off-piste, rescue is undertaken by the P.G.H.M. (Mountain rescue).

LES PISTES / *THE RUNS*

a - Piste « Charles Bozon », noire / *black*

b - Piste « Combe des Vioz », bleue / *blue*

c - Piste 2000, verte / *green*

d - Piste de liaison, verte / *linking piste, green*

e - Piste du Stade, bleue, (compétitions), *competition piste, blue*

f - Piste du Blanchot, bleue / *blue*

g - Piste du Pain de Sucre, bleue / *blue*

h - Piste du Col Cornu, rouge / *red* (longueur: 4500 m) / *(length: 4500 m)*

i - Piste des Chamois, noire / *black*

j - Piste de la Combe de la Charlanon, rouge / *red*

k - Piste des Bouquetins, noire / *black*

l - Piste des Tétras, rouge / *red*

m - Piste de la Source, rouge / *red*

n - Piste des Nants, noire / *black*

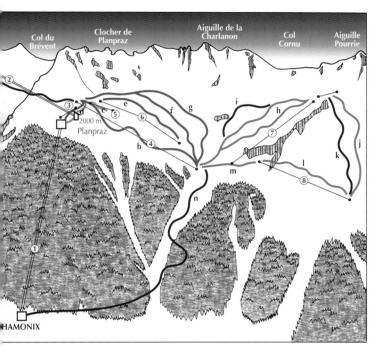

1. Télécabine Chamonix-Planpraz   (1095 m - 2000 m)   - 1350 pers./h.

2. Téléphérique Planparz-Brévent   (2000 m - 2525 m)   - 900 pers./h

3. Télésiège Altitude 2000   (2000 m - 2700 m)   - 1200 pers./h.

4. Télésiège de La Parsa   (1800 m - 2070 m)   - 1800 pers./h.

5. Téléski Altitude 2000   (déniv. 60 m)   - 500 pers./h.

6. Téléski du Stade   (déniv. 180 m)   - 900 pers./h.

7. Télésiège du Col Cornu   (1800 m - 2350 m)   - 1350 pers./h.

8. Télésiège de la Charlanon   (1650 m - 2000 m)   - 900 pers./h.

BELLACHAT

Une superbe descente, de grande envergure, très variée. Les pentes du haut, larges et soutenues, sont fabuleuses en neige de printemps. Le bas, sur un chemin scabreux, dans la forêt, fait bonne figure au rayon "ski de combat".

- **Dénivellation** : 1500 m.
- **Exposition** : sud.
- **Dif. technique** : Difficile; pentes jusqu'à 35°/40°.
- **Engagement** : très engagé.
- **Dangers** : risque de dévissage non négligeable; pentes propices aux plaques à vent; traversée de plusieurs couloirs d'avalanche.
- **Cheminement** : complexe; temps sûr indispensable.
- **Période propice** : début de printemps, quand la neige est transformée, et qu'il reste suffisamment de neige pour rejoindre Chamonix à skis.

- **Itinéraire** : du sommet du téléphérique du Brévent, quitter, après une cinquantaine de mètres, la piste pour bifurquer à gauche en direction de l'Aiguillette des Houches. Par de larges pentes (attention: pierres!) gagner en tirant progressivement à gauche un rétrécissement qui permet d'atteindre une combe, que l'on traverse pour rejoindre l'arête sud du Brévent. Suivre cette arête pendant environ 800 m, pratiquement à l'horizontale, jusqu'à l'aplomb du refuge de Bellachat, visible sur l'autre versant. (On peut également s'engager dans la descente en amont par un large couloir, très raide). Descendre alors versant sud, une succession de pentes, soutenues dans l'ensemble, jusqu'à un ressaut plus raide que l'on franchit légèrement sur la droite ("louvoyer" au mieux selon les conditions). Passage de 35°/40°.

On tire alors progressivement à gauche jusqu'à un très large couloir d'avalanche que l'on emprunte, en continuant de descendre en oblique pour rejoindre sa rive gauche.

De l'autre côté, à l'altitude de 1550 m, repérer un chemin qui pénètre la forêt

(ouvrir l'oeil!...). Suivre ce chemin qui fait un grand zig, puis grand zag dans la forêt (sportif...) pour finalement déboucher dans une clairière au-dessus du village des Moussoux.

Descendre dans cette clairière en continuant de tirer à gauche jusqu'à la route. La traverser et continuer horizontalement - lieu-dit "les Moettieux" - jusqu'au parking de la télécabine de Planpraz.

BELLACHAT

A superb run, wide ranging and varied. Up top, the slopes are large and sustained, fabulous on spring snow. The bottom, on a scabby track through the forest, is pretty much "combat skiing".

- *Vertical drop*   : 1500 m.
- *Exposition*   : south facing.
- *Technical diff.*   : Difficult: slopes up to 35°/40°.
- *Commitment*   : very serious.
- *Dangers*   : long slides are possible; slopes exposed to windslab; traversing through many avalanche couloirs.
- *Route finding*   : complex; good weather imperative.
- *Suitable period*   : early spring when the snow is transformed, and there is enough left to reach Chamonix on skis.

- *Route description* : from the summit of the Brevent cable-car, leave the piste after 50 metres in the direction of the Aiguillette des Houches. Across wide slopes (watch out for rocks) attain, on pulling progressively to the left a narrowing from where one joins a bowl. Traverse this bowl to reach the south ridge of the Brevent. Follow this ridge for 800 m, practically horizontal until one is in a direct line with the Bellachat refuge. (One can also tackle off the descent by a wide couloir, very steep).

Now, go down to the south on a succession of slopes, on the whole sustained, until a steep roll, which is passed slightly on the right (check it out according to the conditions). Passage at 35°/40°.

From here, pull progressively to the left until you reach a very wide avalanche couloir. Take this, descending always left to reach the left bank.

Once on the other side, at an altitude of 1550 m, search for a track entering the forest (open your eyes!). Follow this track (a big zigzag, sporting) to finally spew out into the clearings above the village of Moussoux.

Ski down this open terrain on pulling to the left until the road. Cross the road and continue horizontally to the parking of the Planpraz telecabine.

LES GRANDS COULOIRS

Quatre couloirs d'anthologie, qui ont fait la légende du Brévent. On y accède depuis le téléphérique Planpraz - Brévent, sauf pour le Bozon qui se rejoint depuis le sommet des Vioz.

Les quatre couloirs se jettent dans la large combe du Brévent, paradis des avalanches de gros calibres...

THE MAIN COULOIRS

Four historical couloirs, which have helped shape the Brevent legend. One reaches them from the Planpraz - Brevent cable-car, except for the Bozon, which is reached from the summit of the Vioz.

The four couloirs empty into the wide Brevent bowl, paradise for heavy calibre avalanches...

De gauche à droite, sur la photo ci-contre:
From left to right on the accompagning photo:
1. Le couloir de l'E.N.S.A.
2. Le couloir Bellin
3. Le couloir Allais
4. Le couloir Bozon

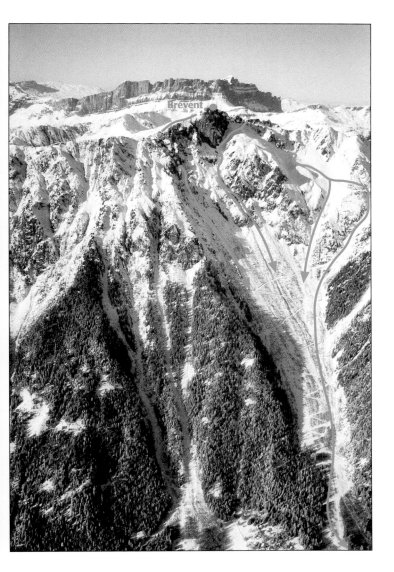

Le couloir de l'ENSA

Le plus difficile. Grande ambiance. Un couloir encaissé, très raide au départ (42°). Baptisé ainsi parce qu'il fut descendu pour la première fois par deux professeurs de l'Ecole Nationale de Ski et d'Alpinisme (E.N.S.A.), Roger ANGE-LIER et Gaston VILLARD, dans les années 50.

- **Dénivellation** : 1500 m; 400 m de couloir proprement dit.
- **Exposition** : est, puis sud-est.
- **Dif. technique** : Très Difficile; pour très bons skieurs ayant une solide expérience du ski de couloir.
- **Engagement** : itinéraire engagé.
- **Dangers** : le risque de dévissage est extrêmement sérieux; par ailleurs l'encaissement du couloir le protège du soleil,et fait que les conditions de neige y sont souvent différentes des autres secteurs du Brévent. Neige poudreuse fréquente; attention aux plaques à vent et au risque d'effondrement de la corniche sommitale.
- **Cheminement** : accès complexe; cheminement évident ensuite.
- **Itinéraire** : du sommet du Brévent, emprunter la piste sur une cinquantaine de mètres pour bifurquer à gauche, direction Aiguillette des Houches. Descendre la large pente en oblique è gauche (attention pierres) pour rejoindre l'arête issue du Brévent au niveau d'une première brèche bien visible (départ du couloir Beaugey: rappel). Continuer sur le flanc ouest jusqu'à un passage extrêmement raide que l'on descend tout droit (50°; saut de corniche souvent au départ) ou que l'on contourne par la droite, plus facile - il faudra alors remonter quelques mètres; à gauche, une traversée au milieu de blocs de gneiss conduit au sommet du couloir. Attention, corniche probable! .. Accéder au couloir par la droite, ce qui permet en général de contourner la corniche. Une courte pente pas trop raide conduit au goulet d'entrée, lui très raide (40° à 45°, selon l'enneigement); également très étroit, ce qui incite souvent les skieurs à le descendre en escalier. 25 mètres plus bas, la pente s'élargit et devient nettement moins raide. Suivre alors le couloir qui effectue en son milieu un coude sur la droite pour venir se fondre dans la Combe du Brévent. Suivre celle-ci jusqu'à Chamonix, en bifurquant à gauche tout en bas, lorsque l'on bute contre la forêt, pour rejoindre le parking de la télécabine de Planpraz.

E.N.S.A. couloir

*T*he most difficult. Ambiance guaranteed. A slotted couloir, very steep at the top (42°). So named because it was skied for the first time by two members of the National School of Ski and Alpinism. (E.N.S.A.), Roger ANGELIER and Gaston VILLARD, in the 1950's.

- *Vertical drop* : 1500 m; 400 m in the couloir itself.
- *Exposition* : east and then south-east.
- *Technical diff.* : Very Difficult; for very good skiers with a solid experience of steep couloirs.
- *Commitment* : very serious.
- *Dangers* : the risk of sliding is extremely high. In places the couloir is so narrow it's hidden from the sun, which makes the snow conditions often different to the other Brevent sectors. Powder snow conditions frequent; watch out for windslab and take care at the summit cornice.
- *Access* : complicated, once in the couloir obvious.
- *Route description* : from the summit of the Brevent, take the piste for 50 m then left direction Aiguillette des Houches. Descend the wide slope traversing to the left (watch out for rocks) to reach the arete coming from the Brevent at the same height as the first easily visible breach (top of the Beaugey couloir). Continue on the west flank until a very steep passage which is skied down directly (50°, often a cornice jump at the top) or contoured on the right, easier. From here climb up several metres; to the left a rising traverse among blocks of gneiss leads one to the summit of the couloir.

Watch out for a probable cornice. Drop into the couloir by the right, which usually allows one to avoid the cornice. A short, not too steep slope leads to the entry gully, itself very steep (40° - 45° according to the conditions), also very narrow, which often incites the skiers to step down. 25 metres further down, the slope widens and becomes clearly less steep. Follow then the couloir, which makes a dog-leg in the middle to finally arrive in the main Brevent bowl. Descend the bowl until Chamonix, pulling to the left on reaching the forest, to get to the car-park of the Planpraz telecabine.

Le couloir Bellin

Juste sous le téléphérique, un couloir impressionnant qui "tourne" dans sa partie centrale (un accident mortel a déjà eu lieu à cet endroit). La première partie, sous la muraille du Brévent, est particulièrement belle. Porte le nom de son précurseur, le fameux Fernand BELLIN, guide et cabinier de choc qui n'hésitait pas à sortir de la cabine du téléphérique Planpraz-Brévent, en plein parcours, pour s'offrir un petit tour de benne par l'extérieur, sous le regard incrédule et terrorisé des voyageurs.

- **Dénivellation**   : 1500 m; 400 mètres de couloir proprement dit.
- **Exposition**   : sud-est.
- **Dif. technique**   : Très Difficile; ressaut à 40°.
- **Engagement**   : assez engagé.
- **Dangers**   : risque de dévissage extrêmement sérieux. Possibilité de plaque à vent dans le cône d'entrée du couloir.
- **Cheminement**   : assez complexe au centre du couloir; le bon passage est toutefois logique.
- **Itinéraire** : du sommet du Brévent suivre la piste noire "Charles Bozon" pour passer la brèche qui conduit au versant est. On continue sur la piste par une traversée à droite qui conduit à une sorte de croupe, sous la muraille du Brévent.

Ici plonge le couloir, le long de la paroi.

Se tenir sur la gauche. Au centre, deux petits décrochements raides permettent de revenir à gauche pour éviter des barres. La ligne continue sur la gauche.

On rejoint en bas du couloir, la Combe du Brévent, que l'on descend directement. Lorsqu'on bute contre la forêt, tirer à gauche pour rejoindre le parking de la télécabine de Planpraz.

The Bellin couloir

*J*ust under the cable-car, an impressive gully which twists in the middle part (already one mortal accident in this place). The first section, under the Brevent wall, is particularly beautiful. First descent: Fernand BELLIN.

- *Vertical drop*   : 1500 m; 400 m in the couloir itself.
- *Exposition*   : south-east.
- *Technical diff.*   : Very Difficult; passage at 40°.
- *Commitment*   : quite serious.
- *Dangers*   : risk of sliding is extreme. Possibility of windslab on the snow-cone which forms the entry to the couloir.
- *Route finding*   : quite complex in the middle of the gully. Yet, the right passage is logical at all times.
- *Route description* : from the top of the Brevent follow the "black" piste "Charles Bozon" and pass the col which leads to the east side. Continue on the piste by traversing to the right, which leads one to a sort of brow, under the Brevent wall.

From here the couloir plunges down, down,...

Keep on the left. In the middle part of the couloir, two small passages lead one to the left, to avoid the bluffs. The line continues on the left. Once in the Brevent Bowl, the descent is the same as for the E.N.S.A. couloir.

Le couloir Allais

Inauguré par le célèbre champion Emile ALLAIS, adepte du ski de pentes raides. Un beau couloir, plus court que les précédents, d'une agréable régularité. En neige de printemps, les contre-pentes suggèrent de superbes virages "sur l'aile".

- **Dénivellation**   : 300 mètres de couloir proprement dit.
- **Exposition**   : S.-S.-E.
- **Dif. technique**   : Difficile; pente à 30°/ 35°.
- **Engagement**   : assez engagé.
- **Dangers**   : risque de dévissage à ne pas négliger; possibilité de plaques à vent dans le haut.
- **Itinéraire** : du sommet du Brévent suivre la piste "Charles Bozon" jusqu'en amont du replat qui précède le chemin débouchant sur "Altitude 2000". On trouve alors le départ du couloir sur la droite. Le descendre directement jusqu'à la Combe du Brévent que l'on suit alors (voir couloir Bozon).

Le couloir Bozon

Anciennement piste d'un noir très soutenu, le couloir Bozon est l'itinéraire le plus logique pour descendre de Planpraz à Chamonix. Une belle pente. En souvenir de Charles BOZON, champion chamoniard, vainqueur du slalom aux Championnats du Monde en 1962, disparu tragiquement à l'Aiguille Verte deux ans plus tard.

- **Dénivellation**   : 1000 m tout compris.
- **Exposition**   : S.-S.-E.
- **Dif. technique**   : Difficile; pente à 30°.
- **Engagement**   : itinéraire assez engagé.
- **Danger**   : le risque de dévissage n'est pas à négliger dans la partie supérieure.
- **Itinéraire** : du sommet du télésiège de la Parsa, basculer au S.-E. dans le haut du couloir. On peut aussi le rejoindre depuis le plat qui sépare "Altitude 2000" de Planpraz (départ des parapentistes). Suivre alors le couloir qui s'élargit d'un seul coup dans la Combe du Brévent. On peut descendre celle-ci soit en suivant le chemin qui la parcourt de long en large, soit directement (un zeste de ski de combat). Tout en bas, lorsqu'on bute contre la forêt, le chemin ramène à gauche jusqu'au parking de la télécabine de Planpraz.

The couloir Allais

*I*naugural descent by the champion Emile ALLAIS, adept of steep slopes. A fine couloir shorter than the preceding two, and of perfect regularity. In spring conditions, the walls offer superb "re-entry" turns.

- *Vertical drop*   : 300 m in the couloir itself.
- *Exposition*   : south, south-east.
- *Technical diff.*   : difficult, slopes at 30°/35°.
- *Commitment*   : quite serious.
- *Dangers*   : don't ignore the risk of sliding, windslab possible high up.
- *Route description* : from the summit of the Brevent, follow the "Charles Bozon" piste until a slight rise preceding the track overlooking "Altitude 2000". From here the departure of the couloir is on your right. Ski down directly into the Brevent bowl which is then followed (see couloir Bozon).

The Bozon couloir

*T*he Bozon couloir is the most logical way to descend from Planpraz to Chamonix. A fine slope. In memory of Charles BOZON, from Chamonix, winner of the slalom at the 1962 World Championship, and who disappeared tragically at the Aiguille Verte two years later.

- *Vertical drop*   : 1000 m to Chamonix.
- *Exposition*   : south, south-east.
- *Commitment*   : quite serious skiing.
- *Danger*   : the risk of sliding is not negligible on the upper slope.
- *Route description* : from the top of the Parsa chairlift, to gain the top of the couloir, turn to the south-east. One can also join the couloir from the flat area which separates "Altitude 2000" from Planpraz (Parapente take-off point). Follow then the couloir which suddenly widens into the Brevent bowl. Ski down from here either by following the track which zig-zags down, or directly (combat-ski). Down low, when one comes up against the forest, swing to the left to join the Planpraz parking lot.

LE SECTEUR DU COL DU BREVENT

Un beau secteur pour se perfectionner en ski de pente raide, sur une ligne de crête très aérienne.

Les quatre itinéraires ici décrits se rejoignent depuis le sommet du Brévent et sont sujets à de nombreuses variantes.

Prévoir dix à quinze minutes de cheminement d'accès.

Important: ces passages dominent des pistes de ski et ne sont donc à entreprendre qu'avec un manteau neigeux bien stabilisé.

BREVENT COL SECTOR

A good place to practise skiing on steep slopes, following an airy crest. The four route descriptions described here are reached from the summit of the Brevent and are subject to numerous variants.

Count ten to fifteen minutes access time.

Note well: these passages overlook ski pistes and must not be undertaken except with a stable snow pack.

De gauche à droite, sur la photo ci-contre:
From left to right on the opposite photo:
1. La Demi-Lune
2. Le Faux-Col
3. Le Col du Brévent
4. La Pente de l'Hôtel

La Demi-Lune

Courte descente sur une pente soutenue. Esthétique.

- **Dénivellation** : 200 m de pente raide.
- **Exposition** : S.-E.
- **Dif. technique** : Très Difficile, pente à 40°.
- **Engagement** : assez engagé.
- **Danger** : risque de dévissage.
- **Itinéraire** : du sommet du Brévent, suivre la piste "Charles Bozon" pour franchir la brèche conduisant au versant est. Remonter alors à gauche le long des plaques rocheuses (école d'escalade) pour rejoindre par un schuss une petite combe encaissée que l'on remonte jusqu'à son extrémité. Basculer alors sur la droite, passer entre deux rochers, et atteindre la crête à l'aplomb du couloir (risque de corniches).
  La descente s'aborde par la gauche, sur une croupe très raide, et se prolonge dans le couloir jusqu'à la piste.

Le Faux-Col

Une belle ligne, avec un départ assez impressionnant.

- **Dénivellation** : 200 m de couloir proprement dit.
- **Exposition** : S.-E.
- **Dif. technique** : Difficile, pente à 35°/40° au départ.
- **Engagement** : assez engagé.
- **Danger** : risque de dévissage.
- **Itinéraire** : comme pour la Demi-Lune jusqu'au passage entre les deux rochers. Descendre alors à gauche jusqu'à un replat, au milieu de gros blocs. Sur la gauche contourner des rochers par quelques pas de descente scabreux, jusqu'à une combe que l'on remonte en ascendance à droite direction E.-N.-E. On gagne alors le Faux-Col, bien marqué (la trace continue à gauche en direction du Col du Brévent).
  Aborder la descente versant S.-E. par un passage raide et étroit. Le couloir va s'élargissant, est de moins en moins pentu jusqu'à la piste Bozon.

The Demi-Lune

*S*hort ski on a sustained slope. Esthetic.

- **Vertical drop**   : 200 m of steep slopes.
- **Exposition**   : south-east.
- **Technical diff.**   : Very Difficult, slope at 40°.
- **Commitment**   : quite serious.
- **Dangers**   : risk of sliding.
- **Route description** : from the summit of the Brevent, follow the "Charles Bozon" piste, past the brèche leading to the eastern side. Sidle round on the left past numerous steep rocky outcrops (climbing site) to reach on schuss a small tight bowl. Hold your height through here. After, veer to the right, pass between two rocks to arrive on the crest above the couloir (risk of cornices). Ski down, first on the left following a roll and then into the couloir, following this to the piste.

The Faux Col

A nice line, with an impressive start.

- **Vertical drop**   : 200 m of couloir properly speaking.
- **Exposition**   : south-east.
- **Technical diff.**   : Difficult, 35°/40° at the top.
- **Commitment**   : quite serious.
- **Dangers**   : risk of sliding.
- **Route description** : as for the Demi-Lune until the passage between the two rocks. Ski now to the left, until a flat in the middle of some big blocks. On the left, contour the rocks by stepping down awkwardly, until a bowl that one sidesteps up and across to the right in the direction E. N. E. One reaches then "Faux-Col" or "false pass", well marked (the route continues to the left, in the direction of the col du Brevent).

Start the descent, by a steep and narrow passage, on the southeast side. The couloir widens, and becomes less steep approaching the Bozon piste.

Le Col du Brévent

Agréable itinéraire: classique.

- **Dénivellation**   : 250 m.
- **Exposition**   : S.-S.-E.
- **Dif. technique**   : Assez Difficile; un passage en traversée à 30°.
- **Engagement**   : assez engagé.
- **Dangers**   : risque de dévissage.
- **Itinéraire** : rejoindre le Faux-Col (voir précédemment) où l'on continue de remonter à gauche, toujours versant nord, sous un petit sommet qui sépare le col du faux-col. La pente se couche, puis redescend vers la droite jusqu'au Col du Brévent, dans une sorte de combe. Descendre celle-ci, peu raide au début. Elle tourne progressivement à droite où la pente s'accentue; traverser alors sur la droite, passage assez raide, pour se placer dans le couloir final, large et souvent bosselé, qui rejoint la piste "Charles Bozon".

La pente de l'Hôtel

Une des plus belles pentes du Brévent. Superbe les petits matins printaniers, lorsqu'elle est légèrement dégelée en surface.

- **Dénivellation**   : 300 m.
- **Exposition**   : Est.
- **Dif. technique**   : Très Difficile par l'entrée directe (haut à 40°/45°).
- **Engagement**   : assez engagé.
- **Dangers**   : risque de dévissage dominant; pente propice aux plaques à vent.
- **Itinéraire** : rejoindre le Col du Brévent (voir précédemment). Du col même, remonter à l'est une petite butte, d'où l'on domine tout le secteur oriental des pistes. Gagner le sommet même de la crête.
Descendre alors directement une pente très soutenue; on peut contourner ce passage par une combe nettement moins raide à droite. Continuer par une large pente, puis un couloir sur la droite jusqu'à la piste du Blanchot.

Le Col du Brévent

*N*ice way down, classic.

- *Vertical drop* : 250 m.
- *Exposition* : south, south-east.
- *Technical diff.* : Quite Difficult; traversing on 30° slopes.
- *Commitment* : quite serious.
- *Dangers* : risk of sliding.
- *Route description* : from the Faux Col (see the preceding) continue to side-step up to the left, always on the north side, under a small summit which separates the col from the faux-col. The slope lessens, then drops away on the right in a sort of gully until the Col du Brevent.

Descend from here, not too steep at the start. The gully turns progressively to the right where the slope steepens; traverse now to the right, on quite steep ground, to attain the final couloir which is wide and often bumped up, to reach the "Charles Bozon" piste.

The Hotel slope

*O*ne of the best runs at the Brevent. Superb on spring mornings, when it is lightly transformed into "corn".

- *Vertical drop* : 300 m.
- *Exposition* : east.
- *Technical diff.* : Very Difficult if one enters directly onto the slope (40°/45°).
- *Commitment* : quite serious.
- *Dangers* : definite risk of sliding; slope susceptible to windslab avalanche.
- *Route description* : attain the Col du Brevent (see preceding). From the col itself climb up a small bulge to the east, from where one overlooks all the pistes in the eastern sector. Best to reach the crest itself in fact. After, descend directly a very sustained slope; one can avoid this passage by a small gully to the right (less steep). Continue down a wide slope, then a couloir on the right leads to the Blanchot piste.

SECTEUR COL CORNU

Un agréable hors-piste de proximité mérite la visite de vos spatules aux abords du télésiège du Col Cornu.
Ces courts itinéraires, ne nécessitant pas de descriptions détaillées, sont facilement repérables depuis le télésiège.

Traversée Brévent-Flégère
par le Col du Lac Cornu et le Col de la Glière:

Cet itinéraire permet de relier par les crêtes les deux domaines. Skier la Combe de la Glière en intégrale reste toujours un grand moment de ski qui fera oublier les 15 mn de montée au col.

- **Accès**   : télésiège du Lac Cornu.
- **Dénivellation** : 120 m de montée; 800 m de descente.
- **Orientation**   : ouest, puis est.
- **Dif. technique** : Peu Difficile.
- **Engagement**   : peu engagé.
- **Cheminement**   : assez simple.
- **Danger**   : gros risque d'avalanches après chaque épisode neigeux (traversée sous l'Aiguille Pourrie).
- **Itinéraire** : à l'arrivée du télésiège du Lac Cornu, repérer la cabane des secouristes. Monter à pied en face de celle-ci. Après une première antécime, suivre à droite pour rejoindre le Col du Lac Cornu (15 mn à marcher quand la trace est faite).

Traverser à droite, direction nord, à flanc de l'Aiguille Pourrie, pour atteindre le Col de la Glière. Descendre un premier ressaut assez raide (corniche possible), et skier la vaste combe pour rejoindre l'itinéraire de la Combe Lachenal.

COL CORNU SECTOR

*A*n agreeable off-piste run, not too far off the beaten track, which is worth a visit, accessible from the Col Cornu chairlift.
These short runs don't need any detailed descriptions, being easily found from the chairlift.

Brévent - Flégère traverse
by the "Lac Cornu" and the "Col de la Glière":

*T*his route allows you to link the two ski areas by a high-level ridge traverse. The joy of skiing the "Glière" bowl from top to bottom easily makes up for the 15 min. slog up to the col.

- *Access* : "Lac Cornu" chairlift.
- *Vertical*
  height difference : 120m up / 800m down.
- *Orientation* : west, then east.
- *Technical diff.* : little difficult.
- *Commitment* : not serious.
- *Route finding* : quite easy.
- *Dangers* : high avalanche risk after a big snowfall, notably on the traverse under the "Aiguille Pourrie".
- *Route description* : from the top of the "Lac Cornu" chairlift go down the red "Charlanon" run for a few metres before climbing up, opposite the ski-patrol hut, to reach a rounded ridge. Follow this right to the "Col du Lac Cornu" (approx. 15 min. if the trail has been broken). Head north, traversing rightwards under the "Aiguille Pourrie", to the "Col de la Glière". Descend into the "Glière" bowl by a steep slope (there may be a cornice) and then follow it down until you reach the "Combe Lachenal" and the "Flégère" ski area.

Variante du Couloir Est de l'Aiguille Pourrie (2561 m)

Un bon terrain d'entraînement pour la pente raide.

- **Dif. technique** : D sur 200 m.
- **Dangers** : avalanches après chaque épisode neigeux.
- **Itinéraire** : du Col de la Glière, suivre la ligne de crête jusqu'au sommet de l'Aiguille Pourrie (20 mn). Descendre plein nord deux raides ressauts successifs (40°), puis suivre un des couloirs raides (35°) qui dominent la combe de la Glière.

Variation: East Couloir of the "Aiguille Pourrie" (2561m).

Good practice for steep skiing.

- *Technical diff.* : *difficult for 200 m.*
- *Dangers* : *avalanche risk after each snowfall.*
- *Route description* : *from the "Col de la Glière" follow the crest of the ridge to the top of the "Aiguille Pourrie". Descend the north side (two successive steep sections at 40°) and then reach the "Combe de la Glière" by one of the steep gullies (35°).*

Photo ci-contre / *Opposite photo*:
a. Combe de la Glière
b. Face Est de l'Aiguille Pourrie

Col
de la Glière

Aiguille Pourrie

LA FLEGERE

C'est la station du soleil, des grands espaces et des Grandes Jorasses, juste en face.

Un des rares endroits dans la vallée où, quand la neige commence à dégeler en surface, on peut s'abandonner à de grandes courbes sur les revers des combes et des croupes qui façonnent ce versant des Aiguilles Rouges.

Un réseau de remontées modernes dessert un jeu de pistes variées; avec un petit secteur facile à proximité de la station intermédiaire.

On remarquera une piste rouge au départ de l'Index dont le mur central ferait pâlir plus d'une noire d'autres stations...

Hors-pisteurs, deux musts vous attendent ici: la Combe Lachenal et la Combe des Crochues; ces deux itinéraires, suffisamment larges et pas trop raides, sont accessibles à de nombreux skieurs par bonnes conditions.

Avec Balme, la Flégère possède le domaine le plus propice à la découverte du hors-piste; dans un cadre somptueux, avec vue sur la Mer de Glace.

This is the resort of sunshine, of wide open spaces, and of the Grandes Jorasses, just opposite.

One of the rare places in the valley where, on spring snow, one can really let go on the back sides of gullies and rolls, which are a feature of the Aiguilles Rouges on their eastern aspect.

A choice of modern lifts serve a variety of runs; with a small, easy sector close to the mid-station.

Off-piste skiers, two musts await you: the Lachenal and the Crochues bowls; these two runs, being sufficiently wide and not too steep, are accessible to average skiers under good conditions.

With La Balme, La Flégère provides the most suitable terrain to discover off-piste skiing; in a sumptuous setting, with a view onto the Mer de Glace.

Photo: *Tim BARNETT*

INFOS

Téléphone : 04 50 53 18 58

Situation : à 2 km en amont de Chamonix, au village des Praz, sur le versant sud de la vallée.

Enneigement : bon en haut, se transformant vite dès qu'il y a du soleil. La descente jusqu'en bas n'est en général possible qu'une petite partie de la saison.

Conditions climatiques : station très ensoleillée; attention, en cas de fœhn, le téléphérique peut être fermé (le fœhn est un vent du sud qui arrive droit sur la Flégère via la Mer de Glace).

Cadre : somptueux; vue entière du massif du Mont-Blanc.

Accès : de Chamonix prendre la route d'Argentière, direction la Suisse, jusqu'au village des Praz, à la sortie duquel on trouve le départ du téléphérique.

Restauration : bar-restaurant-self-service à la Flégère (1900 m). Terrasse au soleil. Tél.: 04 50 53 06 13.

Secours : postes de secours à la Flégère et à l'Index. Possibilité d'alerte depuis chaque départ ou arrivée de remontée mécanique.

Renseignements hors-pistes : Consulter les pisteurs à la Flégère.

INFORMATION

Telephone : 04 50 53 18 58

Situation : 2 km up valley from Chamonix, at Les Praz village, on the sunny side of the valley.

Snow conditions : good up top, transforming quickly the moment there is some sun. Skiing all the way to the valley floor is usually only possible in mid-season.

Climatic conditions : very sunny station; attention, the cable-car may be shut in case of foehn (the foehn is a south wind which blows straight onto La Flégère via La Mer de Glace).

Setting : sumptuous; view of the entire Mont-Blanc range.

Access : from Chamonix, take the road to Argentière until Les Praz village. The start of the cable-car is signposted at the end of the village.

Food : Bar-Restaurant-Self-Service at La Flégère (1900 m). Sunny terrace. Tel.: 04 50.53.06.13.

Rescue : rescue posts situated at La Flégère and at the Index. The alert can be given at either end of the lift system.

Off-piste advice : consult the ski-patrol at La Flégère.

LES PISTES / *THE RUNS*

1 - Piste des Praz (noire / *black*): 5000 m

2 - Piste A Index (rouge / *red*): 2500 m

3 - Piste B Index (rouge / *red*): 2400 m

4 - Piste des Evettes (rouge / *red*): 1200 m

5 - Piste de l'Index (bleue / *blue*): 3000 m

6 - Piste de la Trappe (verte / *green*)

7 - Stade de slalom de la Chavanne

8 - Piste de la Chavanne (rouge / *red*)

Col de la Glière

Combe Lachenal

Télésiège des Evettes

LES REMONTEES / *THE LIFTS*

- Téléphérique / *Cable-car* de La Flégère
  (1050 m - 1900 m) : 750 pers./h

- Télécabine / *Gondola* de l'Index
  (1900 m - 2450 m) : 1440 pers./h

- Télésiège / *Chairlift* de la Trappe
  (1740 m - 1910 m) : 1000 pers./h

- Télésiège / *Chairlift* des Evettes
  (1700 m - 1980 m) : 1350 pers./h

- Télésiège / *Chairlift* de la Chavanne
  (dénivelée, 250 m): 1350 pers./h

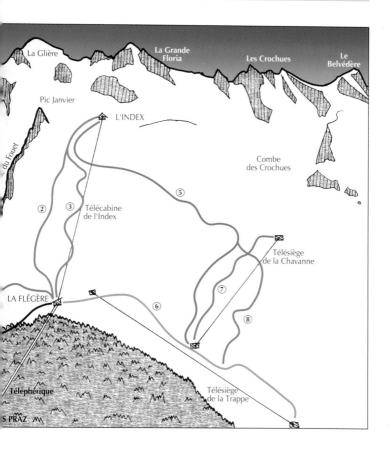

COMBE LACHENAL

Redevenue depuis peu un itinéraire balisé, la Combe Lachenal demeure une des grandes et belles descentes de la vallée. En poudreuse, ou en neige de printemps, ces grands espaces semblent avoir été dessinés pour le ski. Baptisée ainsi en mémoire du célèbre alpiniste Louis LACHENAL, vainqueur de l'Annapurna en 1950, et disparu tragiquement à skis dans la Vallée Blanche en novembre 1955.

- Itinéraire classique
- Dénivellation   : 750 m.
- Orientation   : S.-E.
- Dif. technique   : Assez Difficile.
- Engagement   : peu/assez engagé.
- Danger   : itinéraire relativement sûr, bien que l'ampleur des pentes doive inciter à la prudence en cas d'accumulation importante de neige.
- Cheminement   : peu complexe.
- Itinéraire : du sommet de la télécabine de l'Index, traverser horizontalement vers le sud-ouest pour atteindre le haut de la combe, bien en amont du Pic Janvier, sous le sommet de l'Index. On suit alors cette vaste dépression, raide au départ, qui va s'élargissant, gonflée par la combe de la Glière. De nombreuses possibilités permettent de contourner les petites barres rocheuses de la partie centrale.

Quand la pente s'aplatit, tirer à gauche pour rejoindre un vallon boisé qui conduit au télésiège des Evettes.

Nota: on peut effectuer cette descente en restant bien à gauche tout au long, sur les contrepentes de l'arête du Fouet. Belles pentes.

De gauche à droite, sur la photo ci-contre / *From left to right on the opposite photo:*
1. Les flancs de l'Aiguille Pourrie.
2. La Combe Lachenal, avec son prolongement logique: le couloir des Lanchers.

COMBE LACHENAL (bowl)

*T*he Combe Lachenal has once again become a marked trail and remains one of the great beautiful runs of the valley. In powder, or on spring snow, these wide open spaces seem to have been made for skiing. So named in memory of the famous alpinist Louis LACHENAL who climbed Annapurna in 1950, and who disappeared tragically on skis in the Vallee Blanche, in November 1955.

- *Classic Descent*
- *Vertical drop*   : 750 m.
- *Orientation*   : S.-E.
- *Technical diff.*   : Quite Difficult.
- *Commitment*   : little/quite serious.
- *Danger*   : relatively sure route, remembering that the breadth of the slopes calls for prudence, in case of important quantities of snow.
- *Route finding*   : not complicated.
- *Route description* : from the summit of the Index gondola, traverse horizontally to the south-west to reach the top of the bowl, well above Pic Janvier and below the summit of the Index.

Follow then this vast depression, steep at the top, which then widens, swollen by the Glière tributary. Numerous possibilities exist to avoid the barriers presented by the rocks in the middle section.

When the slope flattens, veer to the left to join a small wooded valley which leads to the Evettes chairlift.

Note: a fine descent can be made, keeping well to the left all along, on the flanks of the arête du Fouet.

COMBE LACHENAL
Les Variantes:

Retour des Evettes / Col de la Poule:

Il est possible de quitter la combe bien en amont du grand plat, par une traversée ascendante à gauche, assez raide, qui ramène sur l'arête du Fouet, à gauche de la tête des Evettes (col de la Poule); suivre cette arête à gauche pour atteindre une raide pente (35°/40°) qui rejoint la piste rouge de l'Index. On peut aussi gagner directement le couloir sous le col de la Poule après quelques contorsions dans des blocs de rocher ...

Le couloir des Lanchers:

C'est le prolongement de la combe Lachenal, rendez-vous des avalanches pour se muscler avant de plonger vers la vallée...

Du plat où l'on bifurque pour rejoindre le télèsiège des Evettes, tirer à droite pour venir aborder le couloir à droite d'une petite crête. Un verrou étroit et raide barre l'accès au bas de la combe; il faut le franchir directement: passage délicat.

La pente devient progressivement moins raide et s'élargit; on reste rive gauche, descendant le couloir d'avalanche (boules fréquentes...) pour finir par atteindre le bas de la piste noire qui ramène à la Flégère.

Cet itinéraire, difficile, ne doit s'entreprendre que par des conditions de neige parfaitement stables, un temps froid, et avec un enneigement suffisant. Se renseigner impérativement auprès des pisteurs.

Les flancs de l'Aiguille Pourrie:

Une belle variante, difficile, davantage exposée aux avalanches; cet itinéraire s'efforce tout du long de rester rive droite de la combe.

Un raide couloir issu des contreforts de l'aiguille Pourrie, permet, le long du bois de Morian, de franchir le verrou du couloir des Lanchers. Plusieurs contrepentes avalancheuses. A n'entreprendre qu'avec d'excellentes conditions et un enneigement suffisant.

COMBE LACHENAL
The Variants:

Retour des Evettes / Col de la Poule:

*I*t is possible to quit the bowl well above the big flat, by a rising traverse to the left, quite steep, which brings one to the "Arête du Fouet", to the left of the "Tête des Evettes" (Col de la Poule); follow this arête to the left, skiing down a steep slope (35°/40°) to join the red piste of the Index. One can also gain directly the couloir situated under the Col de la Poule after a few contorsions in the boulders...

The Lanchers couloir:

*I*s the extension of the Lanchenal bowl, where the avalanches join forces before the final plunge into the valley...

From the flat where one branches off to catch the Evettes chairlift, pull to the right to start the couloir right of a small crest. A steep and narrow passage bars the access to the rest of the gully: unavoidable, tricky passage.

The slope becomes progressively less steep and widens; stay on the left bank skiing down the avalanche couloir (debris frequent) and finish at the bottom of the black piste which brings one back to la Flégère.

- This difficult descent must not be undertaken except with stable snow conditions, cold weather and sufficient snow. Ask the advice of the ski patrol.

The flanks of the Aiguille Pourrie:

A fine variant, difficult and exposed to avalanches, this descent tries to remain all along on the right bank of the gully.

A steep couloir, coming off the Aiguille Pourrie, enables one to pass the bottleneck of the Lanchers couloir, at the level of the Morian forest. Many avalanche paths. To be undertaken only with excellent snow conditions.

COMBES DES CROCHUES

Très belle descente, typique des Aiguilles Rouges; monde courbe, de creux et de croupes, pour un ski très sensuel...

- **Orientation** : S.-E.
- **Dénivellation** : 700 m.
- **Dif. technique** : Peu/Assez Difficile; quelques courts ressauts un peu raides.
- **Engagement** : assez engagé.
- **Dangers** : attention, cette descente domine la piste de la Trappe; elle constitue une menace sérieuse, en cas de neige instable, pour les skieurs, souvent débutants, qui parcourent cette piste verte.
- **Cheminement** : un peu compliqué.
- **Période propice** : printemps.

- **Itinéraire** : du sommet de la télécabine de l'Index, se laisser glisser dans un creux (lac du Fouet) pour rejoindre une traversée à flanc, direction nord-est, légèrement ascendante. Une dizaine de minutes de douce montée en escalier conduisent au sommet d'une bosse qui domine la combe des Crochues. Descendre alors vers la gauche pour prendre pied dans cette petite vallée de rêve. Un plat, une combe à droite, une traversée dans des blocs à gauche et l'on rejoint la tête Aubuy (cabane). Tirer alors à gauche, puis par de larges pentes soutenues, rejoindre le bas de la piste de la Trappe. On peut aussi descendre directement depuis la tête Aubuy.

- **Variantes** :
  De nombreuses variantes sont possibles sur ces vastes pentes. Attention toutefois aux petites barres rocheuses qui peuvent contrarier certains itinéraires. Nous avons tracé sur la photo les deux plus classiques.
  Elles parcourent des pentes plus raides que l'itinéraire normal, notamment la variante la plus à gauche (35°/40°).

CROCHUE BOWLS

*S*uperb descent, typical of the Aiguilles Rouges; world of curves, of bumps and hollows, for a very sensual ski...

- *Orientation*   : S. -E.
- *Vertical drop*   : 700 m.
- *Technical diff.* : little/somewhat Difficult; some short, steep rolls.
- *Commitment*   : quite serious.
- *Danger*   : be careful! This run overlooks the piste de la Trappe; it constitutes a serious menace, when the snow is unstable, for the skiers on this green piste.
- *Route finding*   : a little complicated.
- *Suitable period* : spring.

- *Route description* : from the summit of the Index gondola, slide into a hollow (Lac du Fouet) to join a slightly rising traverse, direction N.E. Ten minutes of easy sidestepping lead to the top of a bump overlooking the combe des Crochues.
  Ski down towards the left to enter this little valley of dreams. A flat, a gully to the right, a traverse through some boulders to the left and one arrives at la "Tête Aubuy" (small hut). Pull to the left, then by skiing down wide sustained slopes, regain the lower piste de la Trappe. One can also ski directly down from the "Tête Aubuy".

- *Variants* :
  Numerous variants are possible on these vast slopes. Always be careful of the small rock barriers which can curtail certain itineraries.
  We have marked on the photo the two classic variants. Here the slopes are steeper than the normal route, notably the variant furthest to the left (35°/40°).

La Combe des Crochues et ses variantes
The Crochue Bowl with its variants

Index

SUITE et FIN

Secteur des pistes:

On trouvera un beau hors-pistes de proximité, facilement repérable depuis la télécabine, en bordure des pistes bleue et rouge de l'Index.

Signalons la succession de petites combes qui bordent le flanc Est de l'arête du Fouet, que l'on rejoint depuis la base du pic Janvier.

D'autre part, deux petits couloirs bien visibles depuis le télésiège de la Trappe, sur la droite en montant, sont propices à la découverte du ski de pente raide. On atteint leurs entrées depuis le plat situé en bas du mur de la piste rouge de l'Index: traverser vers la gauche, passer sous les câbles et s'avancer vers l'Est jusqu'à une masse rocheuse qui sépare les deux couloirs. Pentes à 35°/40°.

Du sommet du télésiège de la Chavanne on peut aussi rejoindre à droite les belles pentes à l'aplomb de la piste de la Trappe (stabilité du manteau neigeux impérative!).

Descentes du bas:

Par un très bon enneigement on peut descendre sous les câbles du téléphérique de la Flégère en veillant bien à tirer à droite pour rejoindre la piste vers l'altitude de 1400 m (barres de rocher au-dessous). Pour très bons skieurs, habitués au ski de combat...

Toujours par bon enneigement, il est également possible de descendre sur la Joux depuis les pentes issues de la Tête Aubuy.

Une série de ressauts assez raides et un cheminement pas toujours évident permettent de rejoindre le plateau de la Chauffria, à proximité de la Joux. Retour aux Praz en train depuis la gare de la Joux. Pour très bons skieurs en forme.

END

Pistes sector:

*H*ere one finds good off-piste skiing close in, with easy access and route finding from the gondola, beside the blue and red pistes of the Index.

Notice the succession of small gullies against the east flank of the "Arête du Fouet", that one reaches from the base of Pic Janvier.

Elsewhere two small couloirs are easily visible from la Trappe chair-lift, on the right looking up. These are perfectly suitable for someone discovering steep skiing. Enter into them from where the red piste of the Index flattens. Traverse to the left, pass under the cables and head east until one comes up against a rocky mass which separates the two couloirs. Slopes at 35°/40°.

From the top of the Chavanne chairlift one can also reach the fine slopes overlooking the piste de la Trappe (stable snow a must!...)

Lower Runs:

*W*ith very good snow conditions one can ski down underneath the Flegere cable-car, well remembering to head right around 1400 m to reach the piste (cliffs below). For very good skiers, used to combat skiing...

Still by good snow cover, it is also possible to reach la Joux by the slopes coming off the "Tête Aubuy".

By a series of steep bulges, and a little bit of route finding, one is led to the Chauffria plateau, not far from La Joux. Take the train back to Les Praz from the station at La Joux. For very good skiers in good shape.

BALME

Le Tour marque le fond de la vallée; petit village typique de la Haute-Savoie, il est dominé par les pentes du Col de Balme où passe la frontière suisse. Ces pentes sont équipées d'un petit réseau de remontées mécaniques desservant des pistes plutôt faciles, très bien entretenues.

Pas de forêt, mais de grands espaces blancs entaillés de profondes combes caractérisent cette extrémité du massif.

La richesse hors-pistes tient beaucoup au versant suisse, lui joliment boisé. Le retour pour certains itinéraires s'effectue en train, après quelques plaques de chocolat et "décis" de Fendant, célèbre vin blanc du Valais.

On trouve aussi de superbes couloirs descendant sur Vallorcine - la vallée des Ours! - haut village authentique du Pays du Mont-Blanc. Ces itinéraires sont aujourd'hui facilement accessibles grâce aux nouveaux téléskis de la Tête de Balme et des Posettes. Une agréable piste facile permet de rallier Vallorcine.

Sur le versant ensoleillé, côté Tour, les curieuses "creuses" de l'Arve séduiront les amateurs de "ski-canyon".

Le Tour marks the upper end of the Chamonix valley; small village typical of the Haute-Savoie, it is overlooked by the slopes of the col de Balme where passes the Swiss border. These slopes are equipped by a small series of lifts serving more or less easy pistes, very well maintained.

No trees, but a big white blanket cut by deep gullies characterise this extremity of the Mont-Blanc range. The off-piste takes place on the swiss side, well forested, by the descent known as Les Jeurs. One returns by train, after several chocolate bars and glasses of "Fendant", a delicious white wine from the Valais (Switzerland)

One finds also superb couloirs plunging down to Vallorcine - Bears Valley! - an authentic mountain village. These runs are easily accessible today thanks to the new T-bars at the Tête de Balme and Les Posettes. A new easy piste links Le Tour with Vallorcine.

Finally, on the sunny side, the quaint hollows in the river Arve will surely seduce the amateurs of "canyon-ski".

Les Jeurs - photo: *François BURNIER*

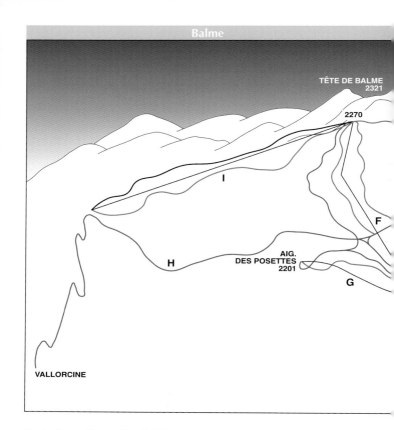

A) Le Tour - Charamillon (1480 m - 1850 m)   1500 pers./h.

B) Charamillon: télésiège - *chair lift* (1490 m - 1935 m)   1350 pers./h.

C) Autannes: télésiège - *chair lift* (1850 m - 2180 m)   1800 pers./h.

D) Arve: téléski - *button lift* (1850 m - 2100)   900 pers./h.

E) Col de Balme: téléski - *button lift* (1930 m - 2180)   900 pers./h.

F) Plan des Reines: téléski - *button lift* (1970 m - 2270 m)   900 pers./h.

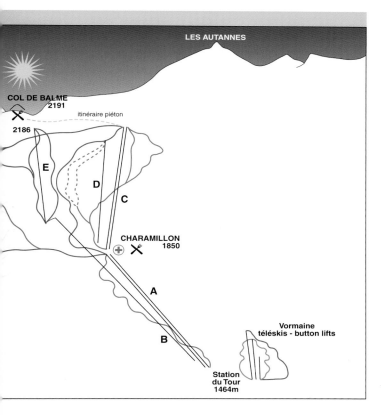

G) Aiguillette: téléski - *button lift* (1970 m - 2200 m)   900 pers./h.

H) Descente sur Vallorcine

I) Esserts: télésiège - *chair lift*

INFOS

Téléphone	: 04 50 54 00 58
Situation	: au fond de la vallée de Chamonix (Chamonix-Le Tour: 11 km).
Enneigement	: excellent dans l'ensemble.
Conditions climatiques	: site bien ensoleillé mais souvent venté; l'ambiance y reste fraîche, ce qui a pour avantage de garder une bonne neige.
Cadre	: très agréable, avec toute la vallée de Chamonix en enfilade.
Accès	: de Chamonix rejoindre Argentière (8 km); 400 m après la sortie du village, prendre à droite. La route s'élève vers le village du Tour. Grand Parking.
Restauration	: bar-restaurant à Charamillon. Tél.: 04 50 54 09 05.
Secours	: postes de secours à Charamillon et au sommet de la télécabine de Balme.

En cas d'accident sur le versant suisse, rejoindre le village du Châtelard et alerter les secours suisses depuis l'une des stations-service (ou rejoindre Vallorcine).

INFORMATION

Telephone : 04 50 54 00 58.

Situation : at the head of the Chamonix valley (Chamonlx-Le Tour 11 km).

Snow Pack : excellent on the whole.

**Climatic
conditions** : very sunny but often windy; the environment remains fresh, which has the advantage of keeping the snow in good condition.

Setting : very agreeable, with the whole Chamonix valley before your eyes.

Access : from Chamonix, direction Argentière (8 km); 400 m after the village, take the right fork. From here follow the river to Le Tour village (3 km). Big parking area.

Food : bar-restaurant at Charamillon, tel: 04 50 54 09 05.

Rescue : rescue posts at Charamillon and at the top of the Balme gondola.

In the case of an accident on the Swiss side, one can alert the Swiss rescue service from one of the petrol stations at Le Châtelard.

VERSANT LE TOUR

Montagne des Posettes, versant sud:

Un agréable parcours en face du glacier du Tour. A savourer en fin d'hiver quand la neige est adoucie par les premières heures de soleil.

- **Accès** : téléski des Posettes.
- **Dénivellation** : 750 m.
- **Orientation** : sud; sud- ouest.
- **Dif. technique** : Peu Difficile.
- **Engagement** : peu engagé.
- **Cheminement** : assez simple.
- **Dangers** : gros risque d'avalanches après chaque épisode neigeux.
- **Timing** : dès la mi-mars, les conditions sont optima jusqu'à 12 h.

- **Itinéraire** : du sommet du téléski, suivre la piste à gauche. Au premier virage, quitter la piste, à droite, plein ouest. Suivre les belles combes sous l'Aiguille des Posettes. Passer en amont des râteliers à avalanche, puis les contourner par la droite.

Suivre une succession de pentes plus soutenues jusqu'à aborder une zone boisée. Au replat (pylône de Catex à gauche), suivre, à droite, un chemin forestier qui domine le village.

Photo ci-contre / *Opposite photo*:
Aiguillette des Posettes versant sud

96

Aiguillette des Posettes

Charamillon

CHAMONIX VALLEY SIDE
L'Aiguillette des Posettes, south side:

A nice descent with a great view over the "Tour" glacier. Best done towards the end of the winter when the morning sun softens the surface of the snow, giving good spring snow conditions.

- *Access*   : "Posettes" surface lift.
- *Vertical drop*   : 750 m.
- *Orientation*   : south; south-west.
- *Commitment*   : not serious.
- *Route finding*   : quite easy.
- *Dangers*   : big avalanche risk after each snowfall.
- *Useful tips*   : from mid-March onwards conditions stay good until midday.
- *Route description* : from the top of the drag lift turn left and follow the piste. At the first bend leave the marked trail and head rightwards (west) to descend through the small valleys and gullies under the "Aiguille des Posettes". Go around the avalanche barriers on their right, and follow a series of sustained slopes which lead down to a wooded area. Reach a flat zone (on the left there is the pylon of an automatic avalanche triggering system) and then take a small track on the right, which overlooks the village, down through the forest to the bottom.

Les Creuses d'Arve:

Les torrents de Charamillon, des Autannes et de Balme sillonnent les alpages et se retrouvent pour donner naissance à l'Arve. Ils forment alors une vallée encaissée, sorte de half-pipe naturel, très agréable à skier ou à surfer.

- **Dénivellation**   : 500 m.
- **Orientation**   : Sud.
- **Dif. technique**   : Assez Difficile.
- **Engagement**   : assez engagé.
- **Danger**   : tout le canyon est fortement exposé aux avalanches issues des Posettes; ces ardoisières génèrent des enneigements très instables. A n'entreprendre que lorsque toutes les pentes sont purgées, et par temps froid.
- **Période propice** : il faut suffisamment de neige pour que les ponts de neige sur le torrent soient solides.
- **Cheminement**   : peu complexe.

- **Itinéraire** : l'accès classique consiste à rejoindre le canyon par une belle pente exposée ouest, en aval du départ du téléski du Col de Balme. On suit alors la gorge, présentant quelques étranglements parfois délicats. En bas on peut, soit rejoindre la piste, soit - s'il y a suffisamment de neige - continuer par le torrent jusqu'au pont en haut du village.

The troughs of the Arve:

*T*he three torrents of Charamillon, Autannes and Balme slice through the meadows, then join to give birth to the Arve.

Further down, they form a tight valley, a sort of natural half-pipe, perfect for skiing or surfing on.

- *Vertical drop*   : *500 m.*
- *Orientation*   : *south.*
- *Technical diff.*   : *Quite Difficult.*
- *Commitment*   : *quite serious.*
- *Danger*   : *the whole gorge is very exposed to avalanches coming off the Posettes: this slatey terrain makes for a very unstable snow pack. Not to be undertaken except when all the slopes have been purged, and by cold conditions.*
- *Suitable period* : *there needs to be enough snow so that the snow-bridges over the torrent are solid.*
- *Route finding*   : *easy.*
- *Route description* : *classically, the canyon is reached by a fine slope facing west, below the starting point of the Col de Balme T-bar. From there, one follows the gorge, which presents sometimes some delicate, narrow passages. Down low, one can either join the piste or, if there is enough snow, ski down to the bridge in the upper village.*

LES COMBES DE LA VORMAINE

Abrité des regards indiscrets, le cirque de la Vormaine offre un large choix de couloirs pour régaler les amateurs de pente.

Nous vous en proposons deux, laissant à votre imagination le soin d'inventer d'autres parcours.

Couloir Nord-Nord-Ouest:

- **Accès** : télésiège des Autannes.
- **Dénivellation** : 750 m, dont 250 m de couloir.
- **Orientation** : nord-nord-ouest.
- **Dif. technique** : Très Difficile. 40°/45° sur 100 m, puis 30°/35°.
- **Engagement** : engagé.
- **Cheminement** : assez simple.
- **Dangers** : gros risque d'avalanches après chaque épisode neigeux. Risque de dévissage en neige dure. Couloir étroit.

- **Itinéraire** : sortir à droite du télésiège des Autannes. Quitter la piste, à gauche, le plus tôt possible. Traverser à flanc, en direction de la base de l'arête de la Tête de Charamillon (rochers). Passer cette épaule, descendre une première pente pour atteindre un large replat. Le traverser, direction sud, en laissant à droite le pluviomètre (structure métallique).

Sur la crête, s'engager dans le couloir offrant le cône d'accès le plus ouvert. L'inclinaison, peu marquée au départ, s'accentue au fur et à mesure que le couloir se rétrécit (45°). Passée cette partie, le couloir devient plus ouvert et moins raide. La fin est évidente: suivre le vallon et revenir à la station.

LES COMBES DE LA VORMAINE

*O*ut of view of the main ski area, the Vormaine bowl offers a large selection of couloirs to skiers and boarders who like it steep. You'll find two different descents described here, but please feel free to choose your own way down.

North-North-West Couloir:

- *Access*   : "Autannes" chairlift.
- *Vertical drop*   : 750 m (of which 250 m is in the couloir).
- *Orientation*   : north-north-west.
- *Technical diff.*   : very difficult. 100m at 40/45° then 30/35°.
- *Commitment*   : serious.
- *Route finding*   : quite easy.
- *Dangers*   : extremely avalanche prone after each new fall of snow; risk of slipping and falling on hard snow; the couloir is narrow.
- *Route description* : from the top of the "Autannes" chairlift head right. Leave the piste as soon as possible, traversing left towards the base of the "Tête de Charamillon" (rocks). Cross the shoulder below these rocks and go down a slope to reach a large, flat area. Traverse it southwards, skiing to the left of the rainfall meter (the metal thingy) to reach the top of the face. From here choose the couloir which is the widest at the top. Don't be fooled by the gentle, upper slopes - they steepen to 45° where the couloir gets narrow. Once through this bottleneck the slopes shallow out and the couloir gets wider. The last part is obvious - follow the valley down to the village.

Photo ci-contre / *Opposite photo*:
Couloir nord-ouest de la Vormaine

La Vormaine

COMBES DE LA VORMAINE
Couloir sud:

- Accès   : télésiège des Autannes.
- Dénivellation   : 700 m, dont 250 m de couloir.
- Orientation   : sud.
- Dif. technique   : Assez Difficile; 30° sur 100 m.
- Engagement   : engagé.
- Cheminement   : assez simple.
- Dangers   : gros risque d'avalanches après chaque épisode neigeux. Risque de dévissage en neige dure.
- Itinéraire : commencer comme l'itinéraire précédent, et passer à gauche du pluviomètre: on skie le long de la crête qui domine les couloirs. S'engager alors dans le vaste couloir orienté sud.

South Couloir:

- *Access*   : *"Autannes" chairlift.*
- *Vertical drop*   : *700 m (of which 250 m are in the couloir).*
- *Orientation*   : *south.*
- *Technical diff.* : *quite difficult (100 m at 30°).*
- *Commitment*   : *serious.*
- *Dangers*   : *extremely avalanche prone after each new fall of snow; risk of slipping and falling on hard snow.*
- *Route description* : *same as above to the large flat area, then ski to the right of the rainfall meter. Ski along the ridge above the couloirs and then down into the large south-facing one.*

A côté des pistes:

On trouve un agréable hors-piste de proximité, propice à l'initiation, le long des pistes. Notamment: de part et d'autre de la piste bleue de l'Arve; à gauche en descendant de la Rouge des Ecuries; et en bordure de la piste Rouge du bas (des Caisets).

Plus sérieuses, les grandes pentes entre la télécabine Le Tour-Charamillon et la Combe de la Vormaine - ancienne Piste Verte - sont superbes. Les rejoindre depuis le chemin qui part plein sud à la gare de Charamillon, devant la terrasse du bar. Peuvent être avalancheuses.

Beside the Pistes:

There is good off-piste to be had beside the pistes, suitable for initiation. Notably, either side of the Arve blue piste; to the left skiing down the Ecuries red piste; and beside the bottom red piste (Les Caisets).

More serious are the superb big slopes between the Le Tour-Charamillon gondola and the Vormaine gully. Reach them from the track which leaves from Charamillon, in front of the bar terrace, direction south. Can be avalanche prone.

COULOIRS DES POSETTES

Plusieurs raides couloirs d'avalanche descendent sur le versant ouest de l'Aiguillette des Posettes, à l'aplomb des petits hameaux de Vallorcine.

- **Dénivellation** : 800 m.
- **Dif. technique** : Difficile à Très Difficile, pentes à 35°/40°.
- **Engagement** : engagé.
- **Dangers** : risque de dévissage; pentes à caractère fortement avalancheux. Ces pentes font partie du P.I.D.A. (Plan d'Intervention de Déclenchement d'Avalanches) aérien, et peuvent être interdites à toute circulation pour permettre un minage par hélicoptère.
- **Cheminement** : assez simple.
- **Accès** : quitter la piste au premier virage de la piste bleue du téléski des Posettes. Traverser en aval, versant sud-ouest, de l'Aiguillette des Posettes pour rejoindre l'arête des Frettes, près d'un gros bloc.
- **Choix des couloirs** : le plus grand - le Praz de Lys - se repère avec évidence (c'est le plus classique). Situez les autres par rapport à lui. Il existe de nombreuses variantes.
- **Sortie** : en bas, couper assez haut pour rejoindre le hameau du Buet, où l'on prend le train (des petits tunnels permettent de passer sous la voie ferrée).
  Attention à ne pas abîmer la piste de ski de fond.
- **Retour** : en train du Buet à Montroc; en bus de Montroc au Tour.
- **Renseignements sur les conditions de neige** : pisteurs à Charamillon.

De gauche à droite, sur la photo ci-contre / *From left to right on the opposite photo:*
1. Les Diets
2. Le Praz de Lys
3. Variante de "la Creuse à Dzorette"
4. Le Rocher des Places - 5. La Creuse des Evirs

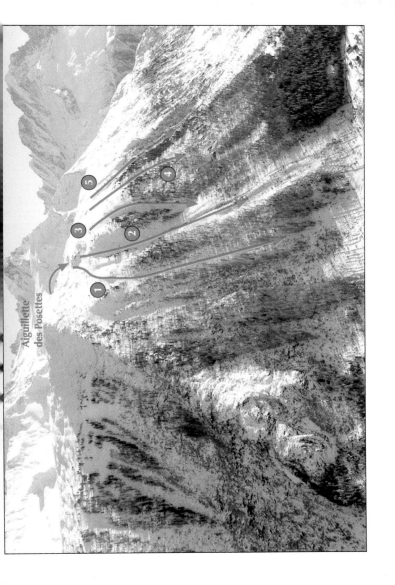

Aiguillette
des Posettes

LES POSETTES COULOIRS

*M*any steep avalanche couloirs plunge down the west side of the Aiguillette
des Posettes, in line with the small hamlet of Vallorcine.

- *Vertical drop*   : 800 m.
- *Technical diff.*   : Difficult to Very Difficult, slopes at 35°/40°.
- *Commitment*   : serious.
- *Dangers*   : risk of slipping, and the slopes are strongly avalanche prone. Sometimes these slopes are closed to allow avalanche control work, by helicopter.
- *Route finding*   : quite simple.
- *Access*   : leave the blue trail of the Posettes skilift at its first turn. Pass below on the south-west side the Aiguillette des Posettes and traverse to the "arête des Frettes", at the level of a big boulder.
- *Couloir choosing*   : the biggest one - Le Praz de Lys - is easily found (most classic). Use it as a reference point. Numerous variants exist.
- *Exiting*   : don't ski the whole slope but cut quite high to reach the railway station at Le Buet, where one takes the train. (Small tunnels allow skiers to pass under the railway line). Be careful not to destroy the cross-country ski track.
- *Getting back*   : by train from Le Buet to Montroc; from there by bus to Le Tour (Chamonix bus).
- *Snow conditions*   : check with the ski patrol at Charamillon.

SECTEUR DES JEURS

Le versant nord de la Tête de Balme offre quelques belles descentes sur un terrain agréablement vallonnée. La trace devra être faite avec intelligence car, ici peut-être plus qu'ailleurs, les coulées sont promptes à partir: ces terrains d'alpages n'offrent que peu d'ancrage au manteau neigeux.

A côté des pistes: on trouve d'intéressantes descentes (dont une partie se situe en forêt) de part et d'autre de la ligne du télésiège des Esserts.

La Combe des Jeurs: d'un accès aisé, la Combe des Jeurs conduit rapidement à l'écart du domaine skiable. Sans être difficile, cette descente comporte quelques courts passages raides, ainsi que des sections exposées aux avalanches.

- **Accès** : télésiège des Esserts ou téléski du Plan des Reines.
- **Dénivellation** : 500 m.
- **Orientation** : nord-nord-est.
- **Dif. technique** : Assez Difficile.
- **Engagement** : engagé.
- **Cheminement** : assez complexe.
- **Dangers** : gros risque d'avalanches après chaque épisode neigeux, avec impossibilité d'éviter les passage exposés. Un des endroits les plus dangereux de la région.

Itinéraire : passer sous le dernier pylône du télésiège et traverser direction nord. Descendre pour rejoindre un vallon. Le suivre jusqu'à un étranglement. Franchir un court et raide passage pour gagner une pente plus ouverte. Suivre cette combe, pour gagner une zone plus plane, bordée à gauche par une crête dominant un cirque.

Deux options sont alors possibles:

1. Entrer dans cette pente raide, à gauche, puis par une longue traversée rejoindre la forêt. De là, poursuivre toujours à gauche, de clairière en clairière pour revenir au télésiège.
2. Ne pas entrer dans la pente, mais suivre la crête. Franchir un premier étranglement formant une sorte de canyon, suivi d'un deuxième. A sa sortie tirer à gauche pour revenir vers la forêt. **A ne parcourir qu'avec des conditions de neige très sûres.**

LES JEURS SECTOR

*T*here are still some great , varied descents to be found here. Think careful
ly about where you're going in this area - it is one of the most prone to
avalanches (the alpine meadows don't provide much for the snowpack to cling
to) and the exact choice of itinerary is crucial.

Next to the pistes: there is good off-piste skiing to be had on either side of the
Esserts chairlift; part of it is through trees.

The Jeurs Bowl: the "Jeurs" Bowl offers some easily accessible off-piste
descents. Although not difficult, these descents have a few short, steep
sections, and are prone to avalanches in places.

- *Access*   : "Esserts" chairlift; "Plan des Reines" drag lift.
- *Vertical drop*   : 500 m.
- *Orientation*   : north-north-east.
- *Technical diff.*   : quite difficult.
- *Commitment*   : serious.
- *Dangers*   : AVALANCHES. After each snowfall these slopes are
                        extremely avalanche prone, and it is impossible to avoid
                        crossing the areas at risk, making this one of the most
                        dangerous places in the book.
- *Route description* : pass under the last pylon of the chairlift and then keep
  traversing northwards. Ski down into a small valley and then follow it down
  to where it narrows. Descend a short, steep section to reach more open
  slopes, and then follow the valley down to a flatter area, bordered on the left
  by a ridge overlooking a bowl.

You now have a choice of two itineraries:

1. Head left down the steep slope and reach the forest by a long traverse.
Continue leftwards through the forest, making the most of the clearings, to
reach the bottom of the chairlift.

2. Don't go down the slope on the left, but keep following the ridge. You'll
come to a gorge which forms a bottleneck. Go down this, and then negoci
ate another narrow section at the bottom of which you head left towards the
forest. **Only to be undertaken when the snowpack is very stable.**

Les Jeurs

Télésiège
des Esserts

1. Combe des Jeurs
2. Couloir de l'Arolette
3. Cirque de Catogne
4. Descente sur le Châtelard

Couloir de l'Arolette

L'Arolette (2338 m) est un petit sommet qui domine le versant des Jeurs. La descente de son couloir nord, combinée avec celle des combes des Jeurs nous donne près de 600 m de grand ski!

- **Accès** : Télésiège des Esserts ou téléski ou du Plan des Reines.
- **Dénivellation** : 150 m de montée (15 à 20 mn) et 600 m de descente.
- **Orientation** : nord-nord-est.
- **Dif. technique** : Difficile. Passage à 40°.
- **Engagement** : engagé.
- **Cheminement** : assez complexe.
- **Dangers** : gros risque d'avalanches après chaque épisode neigeux avec impossibilité d'éviter les passage dangereux. Risque de dévissage dans le couloir. Un des endroits le plus dangereux de la région.
- **Itinéraire** : monter à pied au dessus de la gare du télésiège. Suivre la ligne de crête pour atteindre un premier sommet frontalier: la Tête de Balme (2321m). Effectuer une courte descente, toujours en suivant la ligne de crête, puis gravir l'Arolette, qui est le petit sommet à gauche (5 mn).

Descendre le versant nord, constitué de 2 couloirs encadrés d'éperon rocheux (200 m de couloir). On profite de belles pentes vallonnées qui ramènent aux itinéraires de la Combe des Jeurs.

Photo ci-contre / *Opposite photo*:
Couloir de l'Arolette

L'Arolette

Couloir de l'Arolette

*T*he "Arolette" (2338 m) is a little summit overlooking the "Jeurs" side of "L∈ Tour". Combining its North Couloir with the "Jeurs" bowl gives 600 m o fabulous skiing!

- Access : "Esserts" chairlift or "Plan des Reines" drag lift.
- Vertical
  Height Difference : 150m up (15 to 20 mins.) / 600 m down.
- Orientation : north-north-east.
- Technical diff. : difficult; one section at 40°.
- Commitment : serious.
- Route finding : quite complex.
- Dangers : extremely prone to avalanches after snowfall; risk o falling in the couloir. One of the most dangerous place in the Chamonix area.
- Route description : from the top of the chairlift get onto the ridge and follov it up to reach the summit of the "Tête de Balme", on the border betweer France and Switzerland. Stay on the ridge and, after a short descent, climb up to the top of the "Arolette", which is the small summit on the left (5 mins.) Go down the north side, which has two steep couloirs bordered on eithe side by rocks, (200 m) and then follow the rolling slopes on down to mee the "Jeurs" bowl descents.

Cirque de Catogne

Le Cirque de Catogne est la zone la plus à l'est accessible depuis les remontées mécaniques de la vallée de Chamonix.

Afin de profiter pleinement de cette descente et de ses belles pentes en forêt, nous vous conseillons de poursuivre la descente jusqu'au Châtelard.

- **Accès**   : Télésiège des Esserts ou téléski du Plan des Reines.
- **Dénivellation** : 150 m de montée (15 à 20 mn) et 600 m de descente (1240 m jusqu'au Châtelard).
- **Orientation**   : nord-est.
- **Dif. technique** : Assez Difficile.
- **Engagement**   : engagé.
- **Cheminement**   : assez complexe.
- **Dangers**   : gros risque d'avalanches après chaque épisode neigeux, avec impossibilité d'éviter les passage exposés. Un des endroits les plus dangereux de la région.
- **Itinéraire** : gagner la Tête de Balme (voir itinéraire précédent). Suivre la ligne de crêtes, puis traverser à flanc pour gagner un petit col. Descendre dans le cirque de Catogne. On pourra alors: soit suivre les belles pentes et rejoindre l'itinéraire de la Combe des Jeurs; soit traverser à flanc en direction de belles contre-pentes orientées nord-ouest.

Vers 2000 m, repérer des chalets (2011 m exactement). A ce niveau, il est encore possible de revenir au télésiège par une longue traversée à gauche. Sinon poursuivre jusqu'au Châtelard (voir plus loin).

Cirque de Catogne

*T*he *"Cirque de Catogne" is the most easterly of the areas accessible from the Chamonix Valley ski lifts. In order to make the most of these lovely, wooded slopes, we recommend that you continue the descent down to Châtelard.*

- *Access* : *"Esserts" chairlift or the "Plan des Reines" drag lift.*
- *Vertical*
  Height Difference : *150 m up (15 to 20 mins.) / 600 m down (1240 m if you go to Châtelard).*
- *Orientation* : *north-east.*
- *Technical diff.* : *quite difficult.*
- *Commitment* : *serious*
- *Route finding* : *quite complex.*
- *Dangers* : *extremely avalanche prone after each new snowfall, impossible to avoid the sections at risk. One of the most dangerous areas in this book.*
- *Route description* : *Climb up to the "Tête de Balme" (see previous description). Follow the crest of the ridge and then traverse across the side of the mountain to reach a small col. Ski down into the "Cirque de Catogne", and then either follow the slopes down into the "Jeurs" bowl, or traverse across to ski the north-west facing slopes on the other side. From where you can see some chalets at 2011 m, you can still reach the chairlift by a long, leftwards traverse; otherwise keep going straight down to Le Châtelard.*

Descente sur Le Châtelard

Un itinéraire délaissé depuis la construction du télésiège des Esserts. La partie finale de l'itinéraire se fait à pied, skis sur l'épaule, par un raide chemin forestier qui plonge en fond de vallée.

- **Accès** : Télésiège des Esserts ou téléski ou du Plan des Reines.
- **Dénivellation** : 650 m.
- **Orientation** : nord-est.
- **Dif. technique** : Assez Difficile.
- **Engagement** : engagé.
- **Cheminement** : assez complexe.
- **Dangers** : risque d'avalanches après chaque épisode neigeux avec impossibilité d'éviter les passages exposés. Chemin forestier pouvant être très glissant.
- **Période propice** : s'assurer qu'il y a suffisamment de neige sur la partie basse de la descente.
- **Itinéraire** : au niveau du départ de la grande traversée de retour au télésiège (1950 m), descendre une pente soutenue (bergerie). On skie une trouée dans la forêt qui conduit au réservoir d'eau.

Prendre une route, que l'on quitte rapidement, pour passer un petit pont, à gauche. Traverser, direction nord-est, un large replat et s'engager sur un chemin forestier. Franchir un premier torrent, puis un deuxième. 200 m après ce dernier, obliquer à gauche, dans une clairière, pour trouver un petit sentier. Le descendre skis sur l'épaule. On rejoint la route (20 à 30 mn).

Remonter celle-ci, à gauche, pour gagner le village du Châtelard(10 mn).

Utiliser le train pour revenir dans la vallée de Chamonix (pour Le Tour, faire halte à Montroc et prendre un bus).

Descent to "Le Châtelard"

*T*his itinerary is rarely taken nowadays, due to the prescence of the "Esserts" chairlift. The last part of the descent is by a steep forest track which must be done on foot.

- **Access**   : "Essert" chairlift.
- **Vertical drop**   : 650 m.
- **Orientation**   : north-east.
- **Technical diff.** : quite difficult.
- **Commitment**   : serious.
- **Dangers**   : avalanche prone after snowfall - it is impossible to avoid the dangerous areas; make sure that the snowcover is adequate on the lower section; the track through the forest can be very slippery.
- **Useful tips**   : don't forget your passport.
- **Route description** : from the point where you would normally start the long, leftwards traverse to reach the chairlift (around 1950 m), go down a sustained slope (shepherd's hut) towards the forest. Ski down through a clearing to the reservoir and then follow a small road for a short distance, before leaving it leftwards to cross a small bridge. Cross a large flat area in a north-easterly direction to join a forest track. Follow this down past two streams and then, approx. 200 m beyond the second stream, head down left into a clearing to find another track. Walk down this track to the road (20 to 30 mins). Take the train back to the Chamonix valley (get off at Montroc station to return to Le Tour).

Le Nant Noir

Un superbe parcours de difficulté moyenne qui descend du Col de Balme au Village de Trient.

L'itinéraire, très encaissé, est en permanence sous la menace de coulées d'avalanche venant du versant sud de l'Aiguille de la Croix de Fer. C'est seulement en neige de printemps, quand les conditions de neige sont très sûres, que cette descente pourra être envisagée.

- Accès   : télésiège des Autannes.
- Dénivellation   : 860 m.
- Orientation   : nord-est.
- Dif. technique   : Peu Difficile.
- Engagement   : très engagé.
- Cheminement   : peu complexe.
- Période propice : mars.
- Dangers   : aucune possibilité d'échappatoire. Engager la descente avant que le soleil ne réchauffe les versants sud de la Croix de Fer (au plus tard 13 h).
- Itinéraire : à l'arrivée du télésiège des Autannes, remonter la piste en direction du restaurant jusqu'au Col de Balme (5/10 mn).

Descendre sur l'autre versant du col, en direction d'un vallon, par de belles pentes. Se tenir plutôt rive gauche, pour rentrer dans une sorte de canyon. Le suivre en franchissant quelques passages plus raides. Vers 1500 m, sortir rive gauche pour gagner les prairies qui amènent au village de Trient.

Traverser le village pour rejoindre la route nationale (10 mn).

Retour au Châtelard, soit par le bus postal (se renseigner à la poste), soit en taxi (renseignement au Bar-Bazar).

Le Nant Noir

A fantastic descent of moderate difficulty which takes you from the "Col de Balme" down to the village of Trient, in Switzerland. This route, which follows a narrow valley, is very exposed to avalanches coming off the south-facing slopes of the "Croix de Fer". It should only be undertaken in spring snow conditions when the stability of the snowpack can be properly evaluated.

- *Access*   : "Autannes" chairlift.
- *Vertical drop* : 860 m.
- *Orientation*   : north-east.
- *Technical diff.* : not serious.
- *Commitment*   : very serious.
- *Route finding* : relatively easy.
- *Time of year* : March.
- *Dangers*   : there are no escape routes. Start your descent before the sun softens the snow on the southern slopes of the "Croix de Fer", making them dangerous (ie. before 13h 00).
- *Useful tips*   : don't forget your passport.
- *Route description* : from the top of the "Autannes" chairlift climb up the piste to the restaurant and the "Col de Balme" (5 to 10 mins). Ski down the nice slopes on the Swiss side to reach the valley. Stay on its left bank to enter the gorge and then follow it down past several steep sections. Around 1500 m leave it by its left bank to join the wide, gentle slopes which you follow down to the village of Trient. Cross the village to get to the main road and then get back to Châtelard by bus (information available at the post-office) or by taxi (ask at the bar).

Photo ci-contre / *Opposite photo*:
Le Nant Noir

LOGNAN - LES GRANDS MONTETS

Le téléphérique de "Lognan - Les GRANDS MONTETS", inauguré en 1963, a ouvert un des plus incroyables domaines skiables au monde. Des descentes interminables de plus de 2000 m de dénivelée, une neige abondante gardée au frais, à l'ombre des impressionnantes faces glaciaires de l'AIGUILLE VERTE; le Ski et la Montagne s'écrivent ici en Majuscules.

Du sommet des GRANDS MONTETS, pas moins de trois versants sont desservis: au nord le glacier des ROGNONS avec ses itinéraires multiples, au nord-ouest la raide face du glacier de la PENDANT, et, au sud, le prestigieux PAS DE CHEVRE, qui dévale au pied des DRUS vers la Vallée Blanche.

Le ski hors-pistes resta longtemps une affaire d'initiés, et c'est seulement depuis une quinzaine d'années que LOGNAN - LES GRANDS MONTETS attire tout ce que la planète peut compter de passionnés de grand ski. Un succès qui ne va pas sans conséquences; puisque malheureusement nombreux sont les accidents qui surviennent en hors-piste. La poudre peut être une drogue dure: quand on oublie que la haute montagne impose ici sa loi.

The "Lognan-Les GRANDS MONTETS" cable-car, inaugurated in 1963, opened up one of the most important ski-areas in the world. Of seemingly unending descents with more than 2000 m vertical drop; a snow abundant and well-chilled, in the shade of the impressive ice-faces tumbling from the AIGUILLE VERTE; in one word, MAJESTIC.

From the summit of the GRANDS MONTETS, no less than three aspects await the skiers: to the north le Glacier des Rognons with its multiple possibilities, to the north-west the steep face of the Glacier de la PENDANT and to the south the prestigious PAS DE CHEVRE, which passes under the west face of les DRUS in its head-long rush to the Vallée Blanche.

Off-piste skiing was for a long time here the affair of a select few, but in recent years it has boomed, perhaps to the point of saturation?... A success which is not without its consequences, many are the accidents born from the fact that a cable-car gives easy access to a high-mountain environment, where what one can see, hear and feel is often not enough for safety.

La Face - photo: *Tim BARNETT*

INFOS

Téléphone : répondeur 04 50 54 00 82.

Renseignements personnalisés : 04 50 54 00 71.

Situation : versant nord de la montagne de LOGNAN, village d'ARGENTIERE.

Enneigement : l'exposition nord garantit un enneigement, important et de qualité tout au long de l'hiver, à l'exception de la piste de "LA PIERRE A RIC" qui rejoint ARGENTIERE.

Conditions climatiques : station de haute altitude (3300 m pour les GRANDS MONTETS), froide pendant les premiers mois d'hiver.

Cadre : exceptionnel; le domaine, adossé à l'impressionnante AIGUILLE VERTE s'inscrit au cœur d'un vaste système glaciaire.

Accès : en voiture: depuis Chamonix suivre direction ARGENTIERE (8 km).

En bus : service régulier Chamonix-LOGNAN au départ de l'Office du Tourisme de Chamonix.

En train : Gare d'Argentière.

Restauration : salles hors-sac; self-services; restaurants, bars à la station intermédiaire de LOGNAN et à PLAN JORAN.

Tél.: 04 50 54 10 21.

Secours : permanence secours, LOGNAN, PLAN JORAN, AIGUILLE des GRANDS MONTETS, BOCHARD.

Renseignements "hors-pistes" : poste de secours de Lognan.

INFORMATION

Telephone : 04 50 54 00 82 (answering machine).
04 50 54 00 71.

Situation : ARGENTIERE village.

**Snow
Conditions** : north facing slopes guarantee the quality of the snow-pack throughout the winter with the exception of the piste "LA PIERRE A RIC", relaying ARGENTIERE with Lognan.

**Climatic
Conditions** : high altitude Station (3300 m). The cold can at times be a problem.

Setting : exceptional, glaciated high mountain terrain, dominated by the AIGUILLE VERTE.

Access : by car. From Chamonix, direction ARGENTIERE (8 km); bus: regular service Chamonix-LOGNAN leaving from the tourist office or Chamonix-Sud.

By train : Argentière station.

Eating : picnic room, self-service, restaurants and bars at LOGNAN mid-station and at PLAN JORAN. Tel. 04 50 54 10 21.

Rescue : rescue posts at LOGNAN, PLAN JORAN, AIGUILLE des GRANDS MONTETS, BOCHARD.

**Off-piste
Information** : Lognan rescue post.

LES REMONTEES / *THE LIFTS*

A - Téléphérique Argentière - Lognan
(1230 m - 2000 m) : 750 pers./h

B - Télésiège de Plan Joran
(1230 m - 1920 m) : 1500 pers./h

C - Téléphérique Lognan - Gds Montets
(2000 m - 3300 m) : 450 pers./h

D - Télécabine de Bochard
(2000 m - 2800 m) : 1500 pers./h

E - Télésiège des Marmottons
(2000 m - 2200 m) : 900 pers./h

F - Télésiège de la Herse
(2000 m - 2600 m) : 900 pers./h

G - Télésiège de Plan Roujon
(1910 m - 2150 m) : 1800 pers./h

H - Télésiège de la Pendant
(1800 m - 2150 m) : 1800 pers./h

I - Téléski des Chosalets N. 1
(dénivelée 60 m) : 700 pers./h

J - Téléski des Chosalets N. 2
(dénivelée 25 m) : 500 pers./h

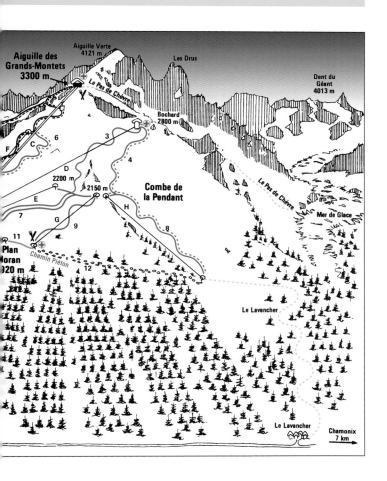

LES PISTES / *THE RUNS*
(plan pages précédentes / *preceding map*)

1 - Piste du "Point de Vue" (noire / *black*): 5200 m.

2 - Piste des "Pylônes" (noire / *black*): 4100 m.

3 - Piste de "Bochard" (rouge / *red*): 3000 m.

4 - Piste des "Chamois" (rouge / *red*): 4500 m.

5 - Piste "Variante de l'Hôtel" (rouge / *red*): 4400 m.

6 - Piste des "Combes" (rouge / *red*): 2200 m.

7 - Piste des "Marmottons" (bleue / *blue*): 1500 m.

8 - Piste des "Arolles" (rouge / *red*): 2000 m.

9 - Piste des "Coqs" (bleue / *blue*).

10 - Piste de "La Pierre à Ric" (rouge / *red*): 3300 m.

11 - Piste de liaison Lognan-Plan Joran (verte / *green*).

12 - Itinéraire piéton / *foot track*.

13 - "Les Chosalets": stade pour débutants / *beginners area*.

SECTEUR: GLACIER D'ARGENTIERE
(photo: page suivante)

Parcouru par la piste du "Point de Vue" (un must) le glacier des ROGNONS, d'orientation nord-est, domine le majestueux cirque du glacier d'Argentière. Les itinéraires hors-pistes sont nombreux, assez difficiles, et réclament une bonne technique toutes neiges, tous terrains. Les crevasses, souvent peu visibles, exigent de rester attentif et maître de sa vitesse. Le matériel de sécurité hors-piste glaciaire (ARVA, pelle, sonde, corde...) s'impose.

Accès   : téléphérique des Grands Montets.
Dénivellation   : 1260 m jusqu'à Lognan, dont 800 m de glacier.

Retour du Glacier d'Argentière (9): suivre dans tous les cas la rive gauche du Glacier. Pour les descentes 1, 2, et 3, une zone très crevassée est à franchir (passage du grand au petit plateau). Installer si besoin une main courante. Hormis cette section, le cheminement reste assez évident. Le retour sur la piste du "Point de Vue" se fait au niveau d'un impressionnant chaos; en franchissant la moraine à gauche.

GLACIER D'ARGENTIERE SECTOR
(photo following page)

With its Point de Vue piste (a must), the Glacier des Rognons on the north-eastern aspect of the Grands Montets dominates the majestic cirque at the head of the Argentière glacier. The off-piste descents are numerous, often difficult and demand good technique in all snow conditions. The crevassed terrain means one must be vigilant at all times, and in control. Security equipment (ARVA, shovel, rope etc.) can be useful.

- **Access**   : Grands Montets cable-car.
- **Vertical Drop** : 1260 m to Lognan with 800 m on the glacier.

- **Return to Lognan (9)**: in every case follow the left bank of the Argentière gla
cier. For routes 1, 2 and 3, a heavily crevassed zone must be crossed (from the
big to the small plateau). A rope can be helpful in early season. Apart from this
section, the route finding is quite obvious. Cut back left to Lognan at the level
of some huge jumbled seracs to join the piste of the "Point de vue".

Glacier d'Argentière, les itinéraires:

1 - Combe du Cordier
2 - Les Rognons
3 - Moraine des Rognons
4 - Combe du Signal Géodésique
5 - Traversée du Dôme
6 - Le Dôme
7 - Pente aux pisteurs
8 - Grand Mur
9 - Retour glacier

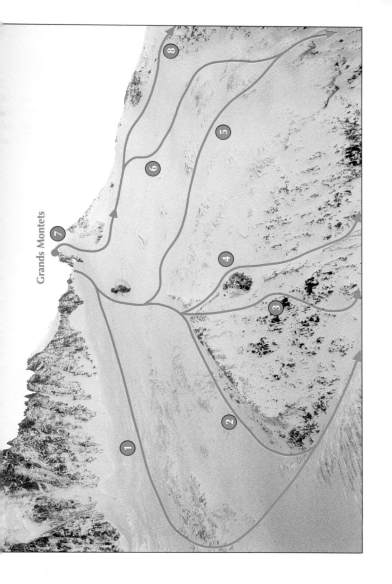

Grands Montets

SECTEUR: GLACIER D'ARGENTIERE
(photo précédente)

1 - Combe du Cordier

- **Exposition**   : nord-est.
- **Dif. technique** : Assez Difficile; pente moyenne et régulière.
- **Engagement**   : engagé. Long parcours glaciaire.
- **Dangers**   : dangers objectifs importants. Fréquentes chutes de séracs qui balaient toute la combe. Ambiance "roulette russe". Nombreuses crevasses.
- **Période propice** : dès que l'enneigement est suffisant.
- **Itinéraire** : passer le col des GRANDS MONTETS comme pour aller au "Point de Vue" et longer direction sud-est les faces rocheuses descendant de l'arête des GRANDS MONTETS. Quand la combe est en vue (à l'aplomb du couloir Cordier de l'AIGUILLE VERTE), la rejoindre par des pentes régulières barrées de larges crevasses. Suivre la combe pour gagner alors le glacier d'Argentière que l'on suivra rive gauche.

POUR SKIEURS - ALPINISTES

ARGENTIERE GLACIER SECTOR
(preceding photo)

1 - Combe du Cordier

Aspect	:	north-east.
Technical diff.	:	Quite Difficult; average and regular slope.
Commitment	:	serious, glaciated terrain.
Dangers	:	high objective danger from serac falls which sweep the whole bowl. Atmosphere "russian roulette". Numerous crevasses.
Suitable period	:	from whenever there is enough snow bridging the crevasses.

Route description : as for the "Point de Vue" then traverse right under the arête des GRANDS MONTETS, holding one's height as much as possible. Descend when in line with the couloir Cordier on the AIGUILLE VERTE (serac fall). The bowl is often cut by large crevasses. Once on the Argentière glacier stay on the left bank.

FOR SKI-MOUNTAINEERS

2 - Les Rognons

- **Exposition** : nord-est.
- **Dif. technique** : Assez Difficile; pentes régulières. La plus accessible descente du secteur.
- **Engagement** : engagé.
- **Dangers** : risques habituels du ski sur glacier (crevasses).
- **Cheminement** : assez évident par beau temps.
- **Période propice** : tout l'hiver avec un bon enneigement; visibilité indispensable.
- **Itinéraire** : descendre la première pente de la piste du "POINT DE VUE" et la quitter à droite, avant qu'elle ne tourne à gauche. Rejoindre alors un Rognon Rocheux caractéristique que l'on évite par la droite (crevasses). Contourner une zone raide toujours par la droite et descendre une belle pente, régulière, jusqu'à une moraine rocheuse identifiable à son signal géodésique. Tirer à droite pour gagner une combe assez raide qui conduit au glacier d'ARGENTIERE. Le suivre rive gauche.

3 - Variante de la Moraine des Rognons

- **Dif. technique** : Difficile. Pentes raides 30°/35°.
- **Dangers** : risque de dévissage. Risque d'avalanche.
- **Engagement** : engagé.
- **Cheminement** : pas toujours évident quand il faut trouver le bon couloir. A observer depuis le glacier d'Argentière.
- **Période propice** : enneigement important et manteau neigeux stabilisé de rigueur (nombreuses pierres).
- **Itinéraire** : du point géodésique, basculer derrière la moraine; suivre une succession de couloirs entre des éperons rocheux et gagner le Glacier d'Argentière.

2 - "Les Rognons"

Aspect	: north-east.
Technical diff.	: Quite Difficult; even slopes. The most accessible descent in this sector.
Commitment	: serious.
Dangers	: crevassed terrain.
Route finding	: quite obvious during fine weather.
Suitable period	: with good snow all winter long; visibility a must.

Route description : quit the piste of the "POINT DE VUE" where it sweeps left. Ski straight down and pass on the right a big rocky outcrop. Avoid again on the right a steep zone to reach a fine even slope. Ski down to a trig station. From here, veer right into a quite steep bowl to join the ARGENTIERE glacier.

3 - Moraine des Rognons variant

- *Dif. technique*	: Difficult. Steep slopes 30°/35°.
- *Dangers*	: risk of slipping. Avalanche possible.
- *Commitment*	: serious.
- *Route finding*	: not always obvious to find the right exit couloir. Observe from the Argentière glacier.
- *Suitable period*	: deep, stable snowpack necessary (many rocks).

- *Route description* : from the trig station, drop behind the moraine wall; follow a succession of couloirs between rocky spurs descending into the Argentière glacier.

4 - Combe du Point Géodésique

- **Difficulté**   : Difficile.
- **Engagement**   : engagé.
- **Cheminement**   : assez évident. Descente à observer depuis le Glacier d'ARGENTIERE.
- **Dangers**   : risque d'avalanche et plaques à vent dans le haut de la combe. Risques de dévissage dans les derniers couloirs.
- **Itinéraire** : une cinquantaine de mètres en amont du point géodésique, tirer à gauche en franchissant une légère crête et descendre une combe raide bordée à droite par un épaulement rocheux. Le suivre jusqu'à ce qu'il devienne moins marqué. Traverser alors à droite pour gagner une succession de couloirs pentus qui rejoignent le glacier d'ARGENTIERE.

5 - Traversée du Dôme

- **Difficulté**   : Difficile.
- **Engagement**   : très engagé. Bon enneigement nécessaire.
- **Cheminement**   : complexe; demande une bonne connaissance du terrain. Une erreur d'itinéraire dans la partie basse du glacier peut se solder par un dernier grand saut... Concours d'un guide conseillé.
- **Itinéraire** : suivre l'itinéraire n° 2 (Les ROGNONS); à mi-chemin, entre le point géodésique et le Rognon, entamer une longue traversée descendante entrecoupée de vallonnements. Une fois à vue d'une zone de séracs plus marquée (rive gauche du glacier), entamer une descente prudente pour rejoindre un passage étroit sous des séracs. Il permet de quitter le glacier (altitude de sortie du Dôme: 2650 m). Longer ensuite la langue du glacier par des combes soutenues qui conduisent au glacier D'ARGENTIERE.

4 - Trig Station Bowl

- *Technical diff.* : Difficult.
- *Commitment* : quite serious.
- *Route-finding* : obvious. Observe the exit from the Argentière glacier.
- *Dangers* : avalanche risk from wind-slab at the top of the bowl. Risk of slipping in the exit couloirs.
- *Route Description*: fifty metres before the trig station, veer left, crossing a slight crest. Descend a steep bowl with a rocky shoulder on the right. When the shoulder becomes less defined, traverse right to pick up a succession of steep couloirs dropping onto the ARGENTIERE glacier.

5 - Traversée du Dôme

- *Technical diff.* : Difficult.
- *Commitment* : very serious. Good snow cover necessary.
- *Route-finding* : complex, demanding a good knowledge of the terrain, especially towards the bottom (very exposed). Guide advisable.
- *Route Description*: follow itinerary n° 2 (Les ROGNONS), to halfway between the Rognon (rocky knob) and the trig station. From here, traverse left until in sight of an obvious serac zone (left bank). Descend prudently until underneath an ice wall and descend the narrow passage below. Follow the sustained couloirs bordering the final tongue of the Rognons glacier onto the ARGENTIERE glacier.

6 - Le Dôme

- **Difficulté**   : Difficile.
- **Engagement**   : engagé.
- **Dangers**   : crevasses peu visibles.
- **Cheminement**   : évident.
- **Itinéraire** : suivre la piste du "Point de Vue" et la quitter à droite avant le premier mur. Plonger dans une combe parallèle à la piste (crevasses accueillantes). Après un large replat, attaquer une deuxième pente en contournant par la gauche une zone de crevasses; il est possible alors de rejoindre la piste, ou de continuer par la fin de l'itinéraire n° 5 pour atteindre le Glacier d'ARGENTIERE.

7 - Pente aux Pisteurs

- **Difficulté**   : Très Difficile.
- **Engagement**   : assez engagé.
- **Cheminement**   : simple. A observer depuis la traversée des Rachasses.
- **Dangers**   : risque de dévissage. Accès dangereux pour les non montagnards. Rimaye.
- **Itinéraire** : rejoindre la plate-forme panoramique au sommet de l'Aiguille des GRANDS MONTETS. Enjamber la rambarde pour suivre une crête rocheuse escarpée (main courante). Chausser les skis, puis longer la crête, versant nord-est; après une centaine de mètres, plonger dans une large combe raide, à droite, qui rejoint la piste du "Point de Vue".

6 - Le Dôme

- *Technical diff.* : *Difficult.*
- *Commitment* : *serious.*
- *Dangers* : *hidden crevasses.*
- *Route-finding* : *obvious.*
- *Route Description* : *follow the "Point de Vue" piste and drop off to the right before the first steep wall and parallel to the piste (man-eating crevasses). After a wide flat, attack a second slope, turning a crevassed area on the left; it is now possible to rejoin the piste, or to continue by route n° 5 exiting onto the ARGENTIERE glacier.*

7 - Pente aux Pisteurs (ski patroller's run)

- *Technical diff.* : *Very Difficult.*
- *Commitment* : *quite serious.*
- *Route-finding* : *simple to get one's bearings from the traversée des Rachasses.*
- *Dangers* : *risk of slipping. Access can be dangerous for non mountaineers. Bergschrund.*
- *Route Description* : *climb to the look-out point at the summit of Les GRANDS MONTETS. Cross the guard-rail and follow the rocky ridge (fixed cable). Skis on, follow the snow-crest on the north-east side, and drop off after a hundred metres into the wide chute to the right. Negotiate the bergschrund and rejoin the "Point de Vue" piste.*

8 - Le Grand Mur

- **Difficulté**   : Difficile.
- **Engagement**   : engagé (itinéraire non glaciaire).
- **Dangers**   : risque de dévissage, pentes avalancheuses.
- **Cheminement** : peu complexe (par beau temps).
- **Itinéraire** : suivre la piste du "Point de Vue" jusqu'au sommet du premier mur. Poursuivre en traversée descendante le début de la crête des Rachasses. Revenir ensuite dans la face pour passer sous le CATEX (câble transporteur d'explosif). Descendre alors une pente soutenue et régulière, L'itinéraire emprunte une succession de combes (à gauche). Rejoindre enfin la piste du "Point de Vue" par des couloirs étroits entre les rochers.

8 - Le Grand Mur

- *Technical diff.*   : *Difficult.*
- *Commitment*   : *quite serious (but crevasse free).*
- *Dangers*   : *risk of slipping, avalanches possible.*
- *Route finding*   : *quite straight-forward (in good weather).*
- *Route description* : *follow the "Point de Vue" piste until at the top of the first steep wall. From here, holding height as much as possible, traverse left passing under the CATEX (wire cable for transporting explosive charges). From here the slope becomes sustained and regular; in the middle section a series of bowls tending left lead to tight, rock-lined exit couloirs above the "Point de Vue" piste.*

SECTEUR DES PYLONES

Ce versant nord-ouest du domaine est formé, dans sa partie supérieure, par les deux petits glaciers de la PENDANT et de LOGNAN.
Le skieur trouvera ici de magnifiques descentes hors-pistes avec la proximité rassurante des remontées mécaniques. Vigilance de rigueur car, sur ce domaine glaciaire, crevasses et séracs restent toujours menaçants et imprévisibles.

- Accès   : téléphérique des Grands Montets.
- Dénivelée   : 1260 m jusqu'à Lognan dont 500 m de glacier.

PYLON'S SECTOR

The north-west side of the ski-area consists, in its upper part, of the two small glaciers of la PENDANT and LOGNAN.
Skiers will find here magnificent off-piste descents with the lift service reassuringly dose by. Remain vigilant, because on this glaciated terrain, crevasses and serac-fall pose a serious threat to one's health.

- *Access*   : *Grands Montets cable-car.*
- *Vertical Drop*   : *1260 m to Lognan including 500 m of glacier.*

Secteur des Pylônes:
1. **Combe des Rachasses**
2. **La Face**
3. **Variante**

Secteur Herse-Bochard:
4. **Combe des Blanchots**
5. **Combe des Améthystes**
6. **Pentes du Derby**
7. **Pente à Fredo**
8. **Triangle de la Herse et Combes de la Chavanne**
9. **Combe à Germain**

SECTEUR DES PYLONES
(photo précédente)

1 - Combe des Rachasses

- Difficulté : Assez Difficile.
- Engagement : engagé.
- Cheminement : assez simple.
- Dangers : crevasses.
- Itinéraire : des GRANDS MONTETS, suivre la piste du Point de Vue, puis la quitter pour passer le col des RACHASSES. Contourner d'abord une pente raide par la gauche, avant de rejoindre une combe bien marquée au pied de l'arête des Rachasses. Contourner les quelques crevasses qui la barrent, puis sortir à gauche quand la combe devient étroite et impraticable. Descendre prudemment une petite crête glaciaire et revenir de nouveau à droite. La combe des AMETHYSTES constitue la suite de cet itinéraire.

2 - La Face (Glacier de la Pendant)

- Orientation : nord-ouest.
- Accès : téléphérique des Grands Montets.
- Difficulté : Difficile.
- Engagement : engagé.
- Dangers : dévissage; exposé aux chutes de séracs; crevasses.
- Itinéraire : des GRANDS MONTETS, partir versant ouest pour accéder à la face par sa partie la moins raide. Revenir ensuite en direction de l'Aiguille. Descendre une pente raide qui conduit à un épaulement dominant un rognon rocheux. Traverser à gauche sous une barre de séracs pour rejoindre une large combe au pied d'une falaise. Revenir dans l'axe de la pente en évitant quelques crevasses. Parvenu au niveau de la piste de Bochard, emprunter un dernier grand mur qui débute entre deux zones crevassées. Cette dernière partie est accessible depuis la télécabine de Bochard.

3 - Variante: passer à droite du rognon et revenir ensuite à gauche.

PYLON'S SECTOR
(preceding photo)

1 - Combe des Rachasses

- Technical diff.   : Quite Difficult.
- Commitment   : serious.
- Route-finding   : quite easy.
- Dangers   : crevasses.
- Route Description : from Les GRANDS MONTETS, follow the "Point de Vue" piste until the Col des RACHASSES. Immediately on passing the col, ski down keeping the rocks on the right to reach a bowl between an ice wall on the left and a granite wall on the right. Negotiate the crevasses which bar the entry into the bowl and cut left once the bowl becomes narrow and impractical. Descend prudently a snowy ridge and cut back again right. From here, at the level of the Herse, the route down is the same as for the Combe des AMETHYSTES.

2 - La Face (Pendant Glacier)

- Aspect   : north-west.
- Access   : Grands Montets cable-car.
- Technical diff.   : Difficult.
- Commitment   : serious.
- Dangers   : risk of slipping; exposed to serac fall; crevasses.
- Route Description : from the GRANDS MONTETS, head west to enter onto the face by the easy option. A sort of terrace leads one back in the direction of the Grands Montets. From here, ski down a steep slope to a shoulder marking the start of a rocky crest. Traverse left under some seracs to pick up a second slope underneath an ice-cliff. Traverse left and down to cross the wide flat leading to the Bochard traverse. A last big slope awaits, flanked by two crevassed zones. This last slope is accessible from the Bochard gondola.

3 - Variant: turn the obvious ridge on the right and ski directly down into a u-shaped bowl to join the Rachasse-Bochard traverse.

SECTEUR HERSE - BOCHARD
(photo précédente)

La télécabine de Bochard et le télésiège de la Herse desservent un vaste domaine hors-pistes. Il représente un terrain de jeu idéal pour parfaire sa technique, surtout quand les grands itinéraires d'altitude ne sont pas en conditions. Les descentes décrites ne sont ni surveillées ni sécurisées, comme pourrait parfois le laisser penser leur fréquentation. Ce secteur doit être parcouru avec prudence après toute chute de neige (plaques à vent).

- Dénivelée   : 1000 m depuis Bochard; 650 m depuis La Herse.

4 - Combe des Blanchots: itinéraire de raccord, évident.

5 - Combe des Améthystes

- Accès   : La Herse.
- Difficulté   : Assez Difficile.
- Engagement   : assez engagé.
- Cheminement   : simple.
- Dangers   : corniche et plaques à vent au départ de la combe après les chutes de neige.
- Itinéraire : du sommet de la Herse, rejoindre à gauche la combe des Blanchots. La suivre jusqu'à son extrémité pour gagner, après un léger replat, une vaste combe. Corniche fréquente à cet endroit. Rejoindre facilement, du bas de cette pente, le retour du Point de Vue.

6 - Pentes du Derby

- Accès   : Télésiège de la Herse.
- Difficulté   : Assez Difficile.
- Engagement   : assez engagé.
- Cheminement   : simple.
- Danger   : risque de dévissage en neige dure.
- Itinéraire : du sommet de la Herse, rejoindre la combe des Blanchots. Puis la quitter à gauche, pour prendre un des trois couloirs qui mènent a la belle pente du Derby.

HERSE - BOCHARD SECTOR
(preceding photo)

The Bochard gondola and the Herse chairlift serve a vast off-piste area. This is an ideal playground to perfect one's technique, especially when the big runs at altitude are out of condition. The runs described here are neither patrolled nor controlled as one might well think, given their frequentation. Ski prudently after any snow-fall (windslab).

Vertical Drop   : 1000 m from the Bochard; 650 m from the Herse.

4 - Combe des Blanchots: *obvious way down.*

5 - Combe des Améthystes

Access	: from the Herse.
Technical Diff.	: quite difficult.
Commitment	: quite serious.
Route-finding	: easy.
Dangers	: cornice and windslab, if entering into the bowl after a snow-fall.

Route-Description :from the top of the Herse, turn left into the Combe des Blanchots. Tend right where the bowl flattens, crossing a broad ridge into the Amethystes bowl. Cornices frequent. Return by the "Point de Vue" traverse.

6 - Pente du Derby

Access	: Herse chairlift.
Technical Diff.	: Quite Difficult.
Commitment	: quite serious.
Route-finding	: simple.
Dangers	: risk of slipping in hard snow conditions.

Route Description: from the top of the Herse, left into the Combe des Blanchots. Join the crest on the left where possible, to choose one of the three couloirs leading to what are known as the "Derby slopes".

7 - La Pente à Fredo

- **Accès**   : télésiège de la Herse.
- **Difficulté**   : Assez Difficile.
- **Engagement**   : peu engagé.
- **Cheminement**   : simple.
- **Itinéraire** : du sommet de la Herse, partir à droite, en suivant la Piste de Combes. A l'entrée du premier mur, tirer à droite pour revenir le long de l'éperon rocheux. Longer alors la fin de la Piste des Pylônes; enchaînement possible dans le bas avec les Combes de la Chavanne, en traversant bien à gauche

8 - Triangle de la Herse

- **Accès**   : télésiège de la Herse (ou de la télécabine de Bochard).
- **Difficulté**   : Assez Difficile.
- **Engagement**   : peu engagé.
- **Cheminement**   : simple.
- **Itinéraire** : de la Herse, amorcer une longue traversée au départ de la piste des Combes. Rejoindre un petit col derrière le triangle de la Herse, puis longer la moraine à droite pour rester dans le triangle proprement dit. Parvenu à un premier replat, au bas de cette pente (gros rochers), sortir à gauche ou à droite, pour suivre une succession de petites combes assez raides (risque de dévissage).

9 - Combe à Germain

- **Accès**   : télécabine de Bochard.
- **Difficulté**   : Assez Difficile.
- **Engagement**   : peu engagé.
- **Cheminement**   : simple.
- **Itinéraire** : tirer à gauche, à flanc d'une pente raide (Pylône de CATEX: Câble transporteur d'explosif) au niveau du replat qui précède le dernier grand mur de la Piste de Bochard.

7 - La Pente à Fredo

- Access : Herse chairlift.
- Technical Diff. : Quite Difficult.
- Commitment : fun run.
- Route-finding : easy.
- Route Description: from the top of the Herse turn right and right again where possible depending on the snow-cover to reach the rock-spur of the Herse chairlift. From here, the descent is obvious. Down low, it is possible to enter into the Combes de la Chavanne, by traversing well to the left.

8 - Triangle de la Herse

- Access : Herse chairlift (or Bochard).
- Technical Diff. : Quite Difficult.
- Commitment : good, fun run.
- Route-finding : simple.
- Route Description: turn right at the top of the Herse, holding height as much as possible, to a small col between the Herse and Bochard. Stay on the Herse side and sidle along the moraine wall to enter in the Triangle properly speaking. When the slope flattens out (big boulders), exit left or right following a succession of quite steep bowls and gullies (risk of slipping).

9 - Combe à Germain

- Access : Bochard Gondola.
- Technical Diff. : Quite Difficult.
- Commitment : not serious.
- Route-finding : easy.
- Route Description: half-way down the Bochard piste, traverse left at the level of a CATEX Pylon (cable transporting explosives). Take the u-shaped gully between the piste and the rocky ridge to the left.

SECTEUR DU LAVANCHER

La construction du Télésiège de la Pendant a permis de désenclaver ce immense domaine. Certains le regrettent. Si les dangers du glacier sont ic absents, le skieur doit se rappeler, avant de s'engager, que "LAVANCHER" signifie avalanche en parlé savoyard. Cette zone est la plus meurtrière du massif.

- Dénivelée   : 1000 m jusqu'au télésiège de la Pendant.
                   1600 m jusqu'au village du LAVANCHER.
- Accès   : Télécabine de Bochard.
- Orientation   : nord et nord-ouest.

LE LAVANCHER SECTOR

The building of the Bochard chairlift has opened up this vast area. Som people regret the fact. The dangers found on a glacier are absent here, bu the skier must remember that "LAVANCHER" means avalanche in the savoyar dialect. Treat the area with the respect it deserves.

- *Vertical Drop*   : *1000 m to the Pendant chairlift.*
                      1600 m to LAVANCHER village.
- *Access*   : *Bochard gondola.*
- *Aspect*   : *North and North-West.*

Photo ci-contre / *Opposite photo*:
1. Pente "sous la Fillot"
2. Les Rochers Rouges
3. Le Lavancher
4. Variante du Couloir
5. Variante des Varosses

SECTEUR DU LAVANCHER (photo précédente)
1 - Pente sous la Fillot

- **Accès** : Bochard (télécabine).
- **Difficulté** : Assez Difficile.
- **Engagement** : assez engagé.
- **Dangers** : risque de plaques à vent dans le haut de la pente.
- **Cheminement** : assez simple.
- **Itinéraire** : du sommet de la Combe à Germain, traverser le petit col situé sur l'arête à Cormat, puis descendre une large pente jusqu'au Plan des AROLLES. Rejoindre ensuite la piste du même nom. S'assurer que le télésiège de la Pendant fonctionne avant de s'engager dans cette descente.

2 - Par les Rochers Rouges

- **Accès** : Bochard (télécabine).
- **Difficulté** : Assez Difficile.
- **Engagement** : assez engagé.
- **Dangers** : risque d'avalanche; risque de dévissage en cas de neige dure.
- **Cheminement** : assez complexe, demande une bonne visibilité.
- **Itinéraire** : de Bochard, descendre directement dans la ligne de pente une section assez raide. Puis tirer à gauche sans aller jusqu'à la dernière combe du LAVANCHER. Suivre alors une succession de combes entre des zones rocheuses. Revenir ensuite à droite, en direction d'une moraine bien marquée, pour rejoindre la Piste des Arolles. Nous laissons aux skieurs le soin de découvrir toutes les variantes de cet itinéraire.

3 - Par le Lavancher

- **Accès** : Bochard (télécabine).
- **Difficulté** : Difficile.
- **Engagement** : engagé.
- **Danger** : dévissage dans certains passages de la forêt.
- **Cheminement** : assez évident.

- **Itinéraire** : de Bochard, descendre directement une pente raide. Puis entamer une longue traversée jusqu'à la dernière combe, sous la falaise. La suivre jusqu'en bas (plateau de la Pendant). Possibilité alors de rejoindre le télésiège de la Pendant (15 mn de marche) ou de continuer jusqu'au village du Lavancher par un sentier forestier entrecoupé de passage raides.

LAVANCHER SECTOR *(preceding photo)*
1 - Pente sous la Fillot

- *Access*   : Bochard gondola
- *Technical Diff.* : Quite Difficult.
- *Commitment*   : quite serious.
- *Danger*   : windslab avalanche a risk on the top half of the slope.
- *Route-finding*   : quite easy.
- *Route Description*: from the top of the Combe à Germain, traverse the small col separating the Bochard from Le Lavancher; then ski a wide slope until Plan des AROLLES. Continue by the piste of the same name. Before starting out, make sure that the Pendant chairlift is functioning.

2 - Rochers Rouges

- *Access*   : Bochard gondola.
- *Technical Diff.* : Quite Difficult.
- *Commitment*   : quite serious.
- *Dangers*   : avalanche risk; risk of slipping in hard snow conditions.
- *Route-finding*   : quite complicated, needing good visibility.
- *Route Description*: from the Bochard, ski directly down the fall-line (quite steep). Veer left under the rocks without going all the way into the last bowl. Follow a series of rock-lined gullies before finally pulling back right towards a well-marked moraine to join up with the Piste des Arolles. We leave skiers to discover all the variants to this route at their leisure.

3 - Le Lavancher

- *Access*   : Bochard gondola.
- *Technical Diff.* : Difficult.
- *Commitment*   : serious.
- *Danger*   : risk of slipping in certain passages in the forest.
- *Route-finding*   : quite obvious.
- *Route Description*: from the Bochard, ski directly down a steep slope. Traverse left under the rocks until the last bowl. Ski down eventually through some trees until a large flat (Pendant plateau). From here, either rejoin the Pendant chairlift (15 mn walk) or continue through the forest to Lavancher village. (Track with several steep sections).

4 - Le Lavancher, variante du couloir

- Difficulté : Difficile; risque de dévissage. Même itinéraire que le Lavancher. Quitter la combe à droite, quand les arbres commencent à apparaître, et descendre un couloir raide.

5 - Couloir des Varosses

- Accès : Bochard (télécabine).
- Difficulté : Très Difficile. Praticable seulement avec un bon enneigement.
- Engagement : engagé.
- Danger : Dévissage dans la partie inférieure du couloir.
- Cheminement : complexe. Cet itinéraire est une variante possible du LAVANCHER.
- Itinéraire : quand le chemin forestier du Lavancher démarre, prendre les pentes, à droite, qui conduisent à un couloir. Revenir à droite sur une croupe boisée quand le couloir n'est plus praticable. Sections très raides.

4 - Le Lavancher, couloir variant

- Difficult : risk of slipping. Same route as for Le Lavancher. Veer right when the trees start to appear and drop into a steep couloir.

5 - Couloir des Varosses

- Access : Bochard gondola.
- Technical Diff. : Very Difficult. Possible only with a deep snow-pack.
- Commitment : serious.
- Danger : risk of slipping in the lower couloir.
- Route-finding : Complex. Is reached from Le Lavancher.
- Route Description : from the start of the forest track, attack the slopes on the right which lead to a couloir. When this couloir becomes impractical, pull to the right again on a woody rump. Very steep sections.

SECTEUR TABE PLAN JORAN

Idéal pour faire ses premières traces en ski toutes neiges tous terrains, ce petit secteur de belles pentes entrecoupées de combes étroites, occupera également une matinée neigeuse, sans visibilité.

- **Dénivellation** : 240 m.
- **Accès** : Télésièges "Marmottons", "Tabé", "Plan Roujon".
- **Difficulté** : Assez Difficile.
- **Engagement** : peu engagé.
- **Cheminement** : assez simple.
- **Dangers** : risque de dévissage sur neige gelée.

TABE PLAN JORAN SECTOR

Ideal for the apprenticeship; this secluded area of fine slopes cut by narrow gullies is a fine choice for a snowy morning without visibility.

- *Vertical Drop* : *240 m.*
- *Access* : *chairlifts Marmottons, Tabé, Plan Roujon.*
- *Technical Diff.* : *Quite Difficult.*
- *Commitment* : *not serious.*
- *Route-finding* : *quite easy.*
- *Danger* : *slipping on hard snow.*

SECTEUR TABE PLAN JORAN / *TABE PLAN JORAN SECTOR*
1. Bosse du Tabé
2. Pente du Pra d'jan
3. Pente du Restaurant
4. Par la Forêt des Jeures
5. Plan des Jeures, retour PENDANT.

SECTEUR "DU BAS" / *BOTTOM SECTOR (The Trees)*
6. Combe de l'E.H.M.
7. Variante de l'E.H.M.
8. Couloir des Bûcherons
9. Couloir Philippe
10. Couloir sous les Câbles
11. Couloir des Fontanes
12. Couloir de la Jeureumaz
13. La Trappette
14. Cruse aux Favres

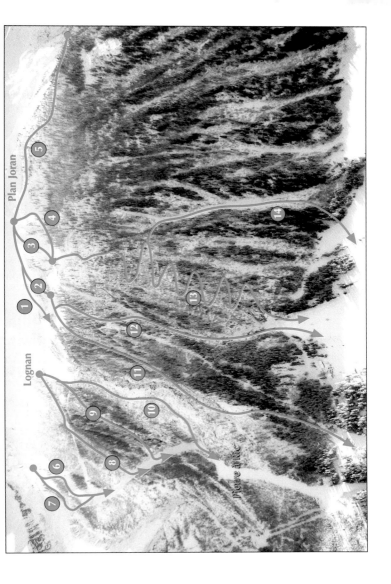

SECTEUR TABE PLAN JORAN (photo précédente)

1 - Bosse du Tabé - Accès et itinéraire : avant le dernier mur de la piste des Marmottons, passer à gauche derrière la bosse.

2 - Pente de Pra d'jan - Accès et itinéraire : suivre la ligne de crête qui borde, à gauche, la piste des Marmottons.

3 - Pente du Restaurant - Accès et itinéraire : suivre le télésiège du Tabé.

4 - Forêt des Jeures - Accès et itinéraire : descendre les pentes dégagées à gauche du télésiège de Plan Roujon pour gagner la forêt de mélèzes. Franchir une succession de ressauts raides et revenir à droite; puis rejoindre le départ du télésiège.

5 - Forêt des Jeures, retour Pendant - Accès et itinéraire : de l'arrivée du télésiège de Plan Joran, suivre le chemin de départ de la piste des Arolles. Descendre, dans la forêt qui la borde, des ressauts pentus. Revenir au télésiège de la Pendant par un bon chemin qui part à gauche.

TABE PLAN JORAN SECTOR (preceding photo)

1 - Bosse du Tabé - *Access and Route Description : before the last wall of the Marmotton's piste, cut left behind the bump.*

2 - Pente de Pra d'jan - *Access and Route Description : follow the crest to the left of the Marmotton's piste.*

3 - Pente du Restaurant - *Access and Route Description: follow the Tabé chairlift.*

4 - Forêt des Jeures - *Access and Route Description: ski down the clear slopes to the left of the Plan Roujon chairlift, to reach the larch forest. After a series of steep rolls, cut back right to the chairlift.*

5 - Forêt des Jeures, retour Pendant - *Access and Route Description: from the arrival of the Plan Joran chairlift, take the track leading to the piste des Arolles. Before the col, drop off at will down some steep rolls. Arriving at a good track turn left to rejoin the Pendant chairlift (some walking).*

SECTEUR "DU BAS"

Les belles forêts qui recouvrent la partie inférieure du domaine proposent quelques descentes de premier choix, empruntant les couloirs d'avalanche. D'une raideur très sérieuse, avec des sections proches de 45°, ces itinéraires sont exclusivement réservés aux très bon skieurs. Des accidents par dévissage surviennent fréquemment à des skieurs inconscients, tentés de suivre une trace, ou attirés par les pentes douces du départ. Rappelons aussi que les jeunes arbres ont besoin de grandir et qu'il convient de faire attention à ne pas les couper avec les skis.

A N'ENTREPRENDRE QUE PAR UN BON ENNEIGEMENT.

- Dénivellation : 800 m.
- Orientation : nord-ouest.

BOTTOM SECTOR

The avalanche couloirs which slash through the forest between Argentière and Lognan provide another dimension to skiing at the Grands Montets. Seriously steep, these runs are reserved exclusively to very good skiers. Accidents from slipping happen frequently to those inconscientious skiers, who are tempted to follow tracks, or attracted by the gentle departure slopes. Remember also that the young trees have a right to grow and that their growth rate is often stunted by ski edges ripping through them.

TO BE UNDERTAKEN ONLY WITH A DEEP SNOWPACK.

- *Vertical Drop : 800 m.*
- *Aspect : north-west.*

SECTEUR DU "BAS" (photo précédente)

6 - Combe de l'E.H.M.

- Accès : télésiège de la HERSE, par la Combe des AMETHYSTES, ou depuis le retour Point de Vue.
- Difficulté : Assez Difficile.
- Engagement : assez engagé.
- Dangers : avalancheux en cas d'accumulation importante. Itinéraire à ne pas parcourir si la piste de la PIERRE A RIC est fermée.
- Itinéraire : repérer le chalet de l'E.H.M. que l'on rejoint par de belles pentes vallonnées. Par une traversée descendante, toujours à gauche, aborder une forêt clairsemée. De là, traverser encore à gauche pour gagner une large combe qui conduit à la piste de la PIERRE A RIC.

7 - Variante de l'E.H.M.

- Difficulté : Difficile.
- Engagement : engagé.
- Dangers : dévissage et avalanches (plaques à vent).
- Itinéraire : du Chalet de l'E.H.M., descendre tout droit en suivant une croupe direction nord. Revenir après deux cents mètres de descente à gauche vers la forêt (ressaut à 40°/45°). Continuer pour gagner un replat qui revient à la piste.

8 - Couloir des Bûcherons

- Accès : piste de la Pierre à Ric.
- Engagement : assez engagé.
- Difficulté : Assez Difficile.
- Danger : ressaut de glace au milieu de l'itinéraire; à ne pas emprunter si la piste du bas est fermée.
- Itinéraire : sortir de la piste, à gauche, après le premier mur; pour s'engager dans une large combe, devenant de plus en plus étroite. Aborder avec prudence la partie finale; contourner à gauche (ou à droite) le ressaut "glaciaire" (cascade). Rejoindre ensuite la piste.

BOTTOM SECTOR *(preceding photo)*

6 - Combe de l'E.H.M.

- *Access* : HERSE chairlift, by the Combe des AMETHYSTES, or from the Point de Vue return traverse.
- *Technical Diff.* : Quite Difficult.
- *Commitment* : quite serious.
- *Dangers* : avalanche risk with heavy quantities of snow. Not to be undertaken if the "Pierre à Ric" piste is closed.
- *Route Description* : attain the chalet de l'E. H. M. (stone building) by way of some pleasant gullies. By a descending traverse to the left enter a lightly wooded area. From here, traverse further again to the left to pick up a wide bowl which is skied to the bottom piste.

7 - E.H.M. variant

- *Technical Diff.* : Difficult.
- *Commitment* : serious.
- *Dangers* : risk of slipping and windslab accumulation.
- *Route Description*: from the E.H.M. chalet, ski straight down a rump direction north. After two hundred metres of descent, cut back left towards the forest (passage at 40°/45°). Continue to a wide flat leading back to the piste.

8 - Couloir des Bûcherons

- *Access* : Bottom piste (Pierre à Ric).
- *Commitment* : quite serious.
- *Technical Diff.* : Quite Difficult.
- *Danger* : passage on ice in the middle of the run (small frozen waterfall). Not to be taken if the bottom piste is closed.
- *Route Description* : quit the bottom piste on the left, after the first head-wall. Ski down the wide gully, which becomes progressively narrower. Negotiate prudently, on the right or on the left, the frozen cascade and exit onto the piste.

9 - Couloir Philippe

(en souvenir d'un ouvrier tombé dedans, au cours de la construction du téléphérique)

- **Difficulté** : Très Difficile (sections à 40°); réservé aux très bons skieurs.
- **Engagement** : assez engagé.
- **Dangers** : risque de dévissage. Avalancheux. Ne pas parcourir en cas de fermeture de la piste de la Pierre à Ric.
- **Itinéraire** : descendre sous les câbles du téléphérique de Lognan en longeant une crête neigeuse. Parvenu au sommet du couloir, franchir les deux pare avalanche qui barrent son entrée. La section la plus raide est dans le haut du couloir.

10 - Pente sous les câbles

- **Difficulté** : Très Difficile. Ressaut très raide. Réservé aux très bons skieurs.
- **Dangers** : risque de dévissage. Avalancheux; ne pas parcourir en cas de fermeture de la piste de la Pierre à Ric.
- **Engagement** : assez engagé.
- **Itinéraire** : suivre les câbles du téléphérique de Lognan, pour gagner une pente raide que l'on descend dans sa partie centrale. Au bas du couloir traverser à droite pour rejoindre la piste.

11 - Couloir des Fontanes

- **Difficulté** : Très Difficile.
- **Engagement** : engagé.
- **Dangers** : risques de dévissage. Avalancheux.
- **Itinéraire** : descendre la belle pente située à droite en descendant de la gare d'arrivée du télésiège de PLAN JORAN. S'engager alors dans le haut du couloir, très raide à cet endroit. La suite est évidente.

9 - Couloir Philippe

(in memory of a work-man who fell into it, during the construction of the cable-car)

Technical Diff.   : Very Difficult (sections at 40°),. reserved for very good skiers.

Commitment   : quite serious.

Dangers   : risk of slipping, avalanches. Not to be undertaken if the bottom piste is closed.

Route Description: ski down under the Lognan cable-car, following a corniced ridge. Arriving at the top of the couloir, negotiate the two avalanche barriers which bar the entry. The steepest section is immediately afterward.

10 - Under the cables

Technical Diff.   : Very Difficult - very steep passage. Reserved for confirmed skiers.

Commitment   : quite serious.

Dangers   : risk of slipping - avalanches. Not to be undertaken if the bottom piste is closed.

Route Description : ski directly under the Lognan cable-car, with a steep section about half-way down. When stopped by a deep canyon, negotiate the broken terrain on the right to rejoin the bottom piste.

11 - Couloir des Fontanes

Technical Diff.   : Very Difficult.

Commitment   : serious.

Dangers   : risk of slipping. Avalanches.

Route Description : ski the slope on the right looking down, from the top of the PLAN-JORAN chairlift. After, attack the couloir, very steep in its top section. The rest is obvious.

12 - Couloir de la Jeureumaz

- **Difficulté** : Très Difficile.
- **Engagement** : engagé.
- **Cheminement** : un peu complexe.
- **Dangers** : dévissage.
- **Itinéraire** : descendre la pente douce et dégagée située à droite, en descendant, du télésiège de PLAN-JORAN. Venir dans la forêt en obliquant vers les câbles de la remontée. Skier d'abord dans une clairière dégagée, puis longer à flanc une pente raide, qui conduit à un petit couloir pentu. Le descendre pour gagner le fond de la combe.

13 - La Trappette

- **Difficulté** : Assez Difficile/Difficile.
- **Engagement** : engagé.
- **Cheminement** : assez complexe.
- **Dangers** : chemin étroit où il peut être difficile de contrôler sa vitesse (en neige dure).
- **Itinéraire** : prendre les belles clairières qui plongent sous le restaurant de PLAN-JORAN. Quand la pente devient plus raide et la forêt plus dense, chercher le chemin étroit de la TRAPPETTE. Le suivre jusqu'aux téléskis des CHOSALETS.

14 - Combe de la Cruse aux Favres

- **Difficulté** : Très Difficile.
- **Engagement** : engagé.
- **Cheminement** : assez complexe.
- **Dangers** : dévissage; avalanche.
- **Itinéraire** : prendre le chemin de la Trappette (décrit ci-dessus), et le quitter dès qu'il s'approche du couloir. Traverser alors une zone boisée, puis descendre un couloir très raide qui mène à la Combe. Parvenu au bas de la descente, sortir à droite, dans la forêt, pour revenir aux téléskis des Chosalets.

12 - Couloir de la Jeureumaz

Technical Diff.	: *Very Difficult.*
Commitment	: *serious.*
Route-finding	: *a little problematic.*
Danger	: *slipping.*

Route Description : *descend a gentle, clear slope to the right looking down, from the PLAN-JORAN chairlift. Enter into the forest towards the lift cables. After a clearing, sidle a steep slope which leads to a steep, narrow couloir tending left, leading into a wide, u-shaped gully.*

13 - La Trappette

Technical Diff.	: *Quite Difficult/Difficult.*
Commitment	: *serious.*
Route-finding	: *quite complicated.*
Dangers	: *narrow track, where it is difficult to control one's speed (on hard snow).*

Route Description : *take the clearings under the PLAN-JORAN restaurant; when the slope becomes steeper and the trees more dense, keep an eye out for the narrow track of the TRAPPETTE. Follow it until Les CHOSALETS T-bar.*

14 - Combe da la Cruse aux Favres

Technical Diff.	: *Very Difficult.*
Commitment	: *serious.*
Route-finding	: *quite complex.*
Dangers	: *risk of slipping; avalanches.*

Route Description : *as for the Trappette, but cut left quite early, crossing a wooded zone, to reach a very steep, tributary couloir (u-shaped). Once towards the bottom of the main couloir cut back right into the forest, to pick up the Chosalets T-bar.*

SECTEUR PAS DE CHEVRE (photo ci-contre)

Le versant ouest de l'Aiguille des GRANDS MONTETS propose quelques itinéraires d'envergure, dont le plus connu, le PAS DE CHEVRE, a fait rêver plus d'un skieur. La MER DE GLACE, qui apparaît quelques 1400 m plus bas et LES DRUS dont l'ampleur se révèle tout au long de la descente sont le cadre de cette belle aventure. Aventure réservée aux skieurs très expérimentés, où fautes de carres et erreurs d'itinéraire seront rarement pardonnées.

- Orientation : ouest.
- Dénivelée : 2200 m jusqu'à CHAMONIX dont 1500 m jusqu'à la Mer de Glace.

PAS DE CHEVRE SECTOR (opposite photo)

The west side of the Aiguille des GRANDS MONTETS offers some splendid runs. More than one skier has dreamed about the best known of these, the PAS DE CHEVRE. The MER DE GLACE, 1500 m below, and LES DRUS, whose greatness reveals itself during the descent, are the setting for this fine adventure. Adventure reserved for experienced skiers, where crossed tips and route-finding errors are rarely forgiven.

- *Aspect* : *west.*
- *Vertical Drop* : *2200 m to CHAMONIX, with 1500 m to reach the Mer de Glace.*

Photo ci-contre / *Opposite photo*:
Secteur Pas de Chèvre:
1. Pas de Chèvre Classique
2. Couloir Central
3. Couloir Rectiligne

SECTEUR PAS DE CHEVRE (photo précédente)

1 - Le Pas de Chèvre Classique

- **Accès**   : téléphérique des Grands Montets.
- **Dénivellation** : 2200 m jusqu'à Chamonix; 1300 m jusqu'au Montenvers.
- **Diff. technique**: Difficile; pente à 30°.
- **Engagement**   : engagé.
- **Cheminement**   : complexe.
- **Dangers**   : en neige dure, les risques de dévissage sont importants. Risque d'avalanche après chaque chute de neige. Crevasses. Ressaut, en glace ou en rocher, possible à la sortie du couloir (se renseigner).
- **Matériel**   : approprié au ski sur glacier.
- **Itinéraire** : des GRANDS MONTETS, descendre le glacier du même nom qui part à l'ouest. Se tenir dans sa partie centrale. Repérer une croupe neigeuse dominant, à droite, une large combe. S'y engager prudemment, puis la descendre jusqu'à un replat, à proximité de rochers (2850 m). Partir à droite, en direction d'une barre rocheuse, et aborder un couloir devenant de plus en plus raide et étroit (court passage à 30°/35°).

A la sortie du couloir, skier la combe du torrent des Grands Montets et, dès 2100 m, tirer à gauche pour passer la moraine. Suivre un premier vallon (torrent du Nant Blanc). Poursuivre à gauche (1950 m) pour gagner un replat qui amène - toujours à gauche - au couloir raide ouvert dans la moraine. Sur la Mer de Glace traverser sans perdre trop d'altitude et rejoindre l'itinéraire de sortie de la Vallée Blanche (Les Mottets).

Conseils: en condition de neige de printemps, démarrer la descente dès que le soleil commence à adoucir la neige (après 12 h). Prudence en cas de nuages en fond de vallée: la sortie du Pas de Chèvre, complexe, risque d'être dans la purée de pois...

ITINÉRAIRE DE GRANDE ENVERGURE.

PAS DE CHEVRE SECTOR (preceding photo)

1 - Le Pas de Chèvre (classic route)

*T*his is the classic way down this side. It can be heaven or hell depending on what time you start your descent!

- *Access*   : "Les Grands Montets" cablecar (3300 m).
- *Vertical Drop* : 2200 m to Chamonix / 1300 m to Montenvers.
- *Orientation*   : west
- *Technical Diff.* : Difficult; a few short sections at 35°.
- *Commitment* : serious.
- *Route Finding* : complex.
- *Dangers*   : on hard snow, the risk of slipping becomes serious. Avalanche risk after every snow-fall. Crevasses. You may have to negotiate a rocky / icy section in the exit couloir.
- *Equipment*   : as for glacier skiing.
- *Route Description* : from the GRANDS MONTETS, descend the glacier of the same name, in a westerly direction. A snowy rump will appear with a wide gully on the right. Go down this (carefully) until you reach a flatter area near some rocks (2850 m). Head rightwards towards a rocky outcrop and then down the gully, which becomes progressively steeper and narrower (short section at 30 / 35°). At the bottom of the gully, ski the "Combe du Torrent des Grands Montets" and at around 2100 m head left to cross the moraine. Follow the valley on the other side ("Torrent du Nant Blanc") and then traverse left again (1950 m) to reach the flat shelf which leads left to the exit couloir. This couloir cuts down through the moraine above the "Mer de Glace" glacier. Once on the "Mer de Glace" stay high and traverse right across to join the "Vallée Blanche" where it leaves the glacier on the left (Les Mottets).

Safety Tips: if the snow freezes hard overnight (spring snow), wait until the sun has softened the surface before beginning your descent (after 12h 00). Be wary of clouds lying in the bottom of the valleys; it would be extremely difficult to find the exit couloir in poor visibility.

WIDE RANGING RUN, OF GREAT SCOPE.

2 - Le Pas de Chèvre par le Couloir Central

Un variante du Pas de Chèvre classique à peine plus difficile, et qui permet surtout de rejoindre plus aisément les belles pentes du Glacier du Nant Blanc.

- **Accès** : téléphérique des Grands Montets (3300 m).
- **Dénivellation** : 2200 m jusqu'à Chamonix. 1300 m jusqu'au Montenvers.
- **Orientation** : ouest-nord ouest.
- **Diff. technique** : Difficile. Passage à 35°.
- **Engagement** : engagé.
- **Cheminement** : complexe.
- **Dangers** : Risque d'avalanche après chaque épisode neigeux. Risque de dévissage sur neige dure. Ressaut, en glace ou en rocher, possible à la sortie du couloir (se renseigner). Crevasses.
- **Matériel** : approprié au ski sur glacier.
- **Itinéraire** : même début que pour le Pas de Chèvre Classique. Au niveau du replat, vers 2800 m, s'engager dans la pente qui part à gauche, après une petite selle neigeuse, sur la droite (2697 m). Le couloir devient de plus en plus étroit et pentu (35°). Après le couloir, poursuivre dans la large combe du torrent des Grands Montets et suivre l'itinéraire précédemment décrit.

On pourra également traverser à proximité d'un éperon rocheux pour prendre pied sur la langue terminale du Glacier du Nant Blanc. Poursuivre la descente à flanc de glacier, puis par la combe du torrent du Nant Blanc. On rejoint ainsi l'itinéraire de sortie du Pas de Chèvre Classique.

2 - Pas de Chèvre (central couloir)

This variation is only slightly more difficult than the classic way down, and allows you to reach the superb slopes of the "Nant Blanc" glacier higher up.

- *Access*   : *"Les Grands Montets" cablecar (3300 m).*
- *Vertical Drop*   : *2200 m to Chamonix / 1300 m to Montenvers.*
- *Orientation*   : *west, north-west.*
- *Technical Diff.*   : *Difficult. Section at 35°.*
- *Commitment*   : *serious.*
- *Route Finding* : *complex.*
- *Dangers*   : *prone to avalanches after each new snowfall; risk of slipping and falling on hard snow; you may have to negotiate a rocky / icy section in the exit couloir.*
- *Equipment*   : *as for glacier skiing.*
- *Route Description*: *start as for the classic descent, but at the flattish area around 2800 m, head down the slope that leads leftwards. After a small, snowy saddle on the right (2697 m) the couloir becomes progressively steeper (35°) and narrower. At the bottom of the couloir, ski down the "Combe du Torrent des Grands Montets" to reach the classic descent (previous description) or traverse left near a rocky spur to reach the bottom of the "Nant Blanc" glacier. Follow the side of the glacier down into the "Combe du Torrent du Nant Blanc" which leads down to near the bottom of the classic route.*

3 - Couloir Rectiligne

Un superbe couloir de 15 à 30 m de large pendant 300 m. Doit être savouré à point: ni trop dur, ni trop mou. Une erreur d'appréciation sur les conditions n'est pas permise.

- **Accès** : téléphérique des Grands Montets (3300 m).
- **Dénivellation** : 300 m environ pour le couloir.
- **Orientation** : nord ouest.
- **Diff. technique** : Très Difficile. Pente à 40° / 45°.
- **Engagement** : engagé.
- **Cheminement** : évident pour le couloir.
- **Dangers** : Risque de plaques à vent dans le cône d'entrée. Risque de dévissage sur neige dure. S'informer pour savoir s'il n'y a pas de cascade de glace à la fin du couloir.
- **Matériel** : approprié au ski sur glacier.
- **Itinéraire** : descendre le glacier des Grands Montets en suivant la croupe qui borde à gauche la grande combe du Pas de Chèvre. Au niveau d'une zone rocheuse (3009 m), s'engager à gauche dans le cône du couloir rectiligne. Le couloir devient rapidement très raide, 45°, et étroit sur 50 m, puis s'élargit avec une inclinaison moins forte (35° à 40°). Une fois passée la rimaye, descendre le Glacier du Nant Blanc et rejoindre la descente du Pas de Chèvre.

Le Couloir des Poubelles:

On pouvait, il y a quelques années, rejoindre le Pas de Chèvre par le couloir des Poubelles, situé à l'arrivée de la télécabine de Bochard. Trop facile d'accès, rarement en bonne condition, l'entrée de celui-ci a été condamnée par un filet.

3 - Le Couloir Rectiligne

*B*rilliant. 300 metres of steep couloir varying in width from 15 to 30 metres. You've got to time this one just right - hit it when the snow is too hard or too soft and you'll regret it.

- *Access* : "Les Grands Montets" cablecar (3300 m).
- *Vertical Drop* : 2200 m to Chamonix / 1300 m to Montenvers (300 m of couloir).
- *Orientation* : north-west.
- *Technical Diff.* : Very Difficult; 45° then 40°.
- *Commitment* : serious.
- *Route Finding* : obvious in the couloir, complex afterwards.
- *Dangers* : beware of snowslab at the entrance to the gully; risk of slipping and falling on hard snow; find out if the bottom of the couloir is under water ice before you commit yourself.
- *Equipment* : as for glacier skiing.
- *Route Description* : go down the"Grands Montets" glacier, following the small, snowy ridge which defines the "Pas de Chèvre" bowl on its left-hand-side. When you reach a rocky area (3009 m) head down left towards the top of the couloir which forms a sort of tunnel. There is a steep, narrow section near the top (50 m at 45°) but then the couloir gets wider and less steep (35° and 40°). Cross the bergschrund (crevasse) at the bottom and then ski down the "Nant Blanc" glacier to reach the previous itinerary.

Le Couloir des Poubelles:

It would also be possible to join the "Pas de Chèvre" itineraries by the "Couloir des Poubelles" (summit of Bochard Gondola). It is rarely in condition however, and the entrance has been fenced off.

L'AIGUILLE DU MIDI

L'Aiguille du Midi, passage obligé de tout séjour chamoniard, reçoit chaque année des dizaines de milliers de touristes. Une réputation qui n'a rien de surfaite tant la nature a pris soin de mettre en scène ici un fantastique spectacle de roc, de glace et de lumière. Le téléphérique de l'Aiguille du Midi ne conduit à aucune piste balisée, mais à un vaste territoire d'aventure et d'émotion. Le visiteur de passage, skieur et alpiniste, sera ici toléré à condition de connaître et de respecter les règles du jeu que l'hiver en haute montagne impose. Un virage de trop, une trace mauvaise, et c'est peut-être la crevasse, ou le dévissage vertigineux.

De nombreux itinéraires de grande envergure sont tracés depuis l'Aiguille du Midi. Si la célébrissime Vallée Blanche reste accessible - par bonnes conditions - aux skieurs moyens, l'Envers du Plan et ses multiples variantes proposent des descentes splendides, réservées aux très bons skieurs. Si votre connaissance de la montagne est limitée, le concours d'un guide de haute montagne sera la solution la plus sûre pour vous accompagner dans ces labyrinthes de glace.

The Aiguille du Midi, a must for every visitor to Chamonix, receives tens of thousands of tourists each year. Certainly worth the visit, for a fantastic show of rock, ice and light. This cable-car serves not even a sole marked piste, but a vast territory of emotions and adventure. The passing visitor, skier or alpinist will only be tolerated here on condition that he or she respects the rules that winter imposes in a high mountain environment. One turn too much, a wrong track taken, and it may be the crevasse, or the horror of the big slide... Numerous routes of wide scope are traced from the Aiguille du Midi. Even if the famous Vallée Blanche is accessible - in good conditions - to average skiers, l'Envers du Plan and its multiple variants are splendid runs, reserved for very good skiers. If your knowledge of high mountains is limited, the services of a guide will be necessary in this maze of ice.

L'Envers du Plan - photo: *François BURNIER*

INFOS

Accès	: par l'autoroute Blanche, sortie à Chamonix Sud.
Téléphone	: 04 50 53 30 80.
Situation	: gare de départ à Chamonix Sud.
Enneigement	: doit être suffisant pour descendre à skis vers CHAMONIX et rendre les glaciers praticables.
Conditions climatiques	: ce sont celles de la haute montagne: altitude, froid, vent. Le fonctionnement du téléphérique en dépend largement. Un panneau lumineux informe le public sur les conditions au sommet de l'Aiguille.
Cadre	: un fantastique spectacle.
Tickets	: en vente aux caisses, avec possibilité de réservation. Distribution de numéros d'ordre en cas d'affluence.
Accès	: par l'autoroute Blanche, sortir à CHAMONIX SUD. Vaste parking.
Restaurant	: bar, self-service, restaurant panoramique au sommet.
Secours	: P.G.H.M.: tél.: 04 50 53 16 89. On peut prévenir au refuge du REQUIN, à la Buvette des Mottets, ou à la gare du MONTENVERS. Couverture GSM quasi complète sur le secteur Mer de Glace.
Renseignement Hors Pistes	: Office de Haute Montagne.

INFORMATION

Telephone : 04 50 53 30 80.

Situation : Chamonix Sud.

Snow-pack : must be sufficient to ski to CHAMONIX and render the glaciers practicable.

Climatic
Conditions : High Mountains. Altitude, cold and wind. A display panel informs the public on conditions up top.

Setting : fantastic spectacle.

Tickets : one-ways on sale with reservation possible. Cabin numbers distributed in case of affluence (you can reserve).

Access : By the highway, exit CHAMONIX SUD. Vast parking-space.

Restaurant : Bar, self-service, panoramic restaurant at summit.

Rescue : P.G.H.M.: Tel. 04 50 53 16 89. One can telephone from the Refuge du REQUIN, la buvette des Mottets or from MONTEN-VERS Station. You can use your mobile phone from almost anywhere in this area.

Off-pist
Infos : Office de Haute Montagne.

SECTEUR PLAN DE L'AIGUILLE

Au départ de la station intermédiaire du téléphérique de l'Aiguille du Midi, le Plan de l'Aiguille, on trouve deux belles descentes souvent en poudreuse: le Pré du Rocher, itinéraire le plus classique, et la Combe des Glaciers. A noter que cette dernière est à proximité d'une zone interdite à la circulation à skis à cause de la présence du Catex de protection du tunnel du Mont-Blanc (petit téléphérique permettant un déclenchement d'avalanche à distance).

Le Pré du Rocher

- Accès   : Téléphérique de l'Aiguille du Midi.
- Orientation   : N.-N.E., puis N.
- Dénivelée   : 1290 m, de 2323 m à 1033 m.
- Diff. technique : Assez Difficile.
- Cheminement   : assez complexe.
- Engagement   : assez engagé; pas de pistes sur ce flanc de la montagne
- Dangers   : terrain propice aux plaques à vent. Pas d'échappatoire possible. Attention aux souches en cas de faible ennneigement
- Itinéraire : du Plan de l'Aiguille, se diriger à gauche en sortant, direction N.-E., puis se laisser glisser dans de larges vallons (pentes peu soutenues au départ) en venant progressivement, par un arc-de-cercle, à l'aplomb de Chamonix. Se faufiler au mieux des clairières (rester toujours à gauche du torrent de Blaitière) pour passer au Pré du Rocher (1600 m); enfin un chemin (à gauche en bas du Pré) conduit au circuit de glace de Chamonix.

La Combe des Glaciers

Mêmes caractéristiques que le Pré du Rocher, sauf l'orientation qui est nord-ouest.
- Itinéraire : du Plan de l'Aiguille, se diriger à droite en sortant (passer sous les câbles du 2ème tronçon) et prendre pied dans la grande Combe située immédiatement à côté du téléphérique. Rester dans la Combe pendant 500 m de dénivelée, mais repérer, à partir de 1850 m d'altitude, trois gros blocs plantés à gauche dans la combe. Au niveau du plus bas, chercher un chemin (Taluté) sur la droite à l'horizontale.
Le suivre jusqu'au circuit de glace de Chamonix.
(Rp. Jean-Pierre MANSART).

A gauche: le Pré du rocher *(left)*

A droite: la Combe des Glaciers *(right)*

Plan de L'Aiguille

PLAN DE L'AIGUILLE SECTOR

*P*lan de l'Aiguille is the mid-station. From here, one finds two great runs, often in powder. Le Pré du Rocher, the most classic, and La Combe des Glaciers. Note that this last is very close to a zone forbidden to skiers because of a Catex, protecting the Mont-Blanc tunnel (small wire permitting avalanche control work from a distance).

Le Pré du Rocher

- *Access*   : Aiguille du Midi cablecar.
- *Orientation*   : north-north-east then north.
- *Vertical Drop* : 1290 m.
- *Technical Diff.* : Quite Difficult.
- *Route Finding* : quite complex.
- *Commitment* : quite serious, no marked runs here.
- *Danger*   : beware of snowslab; no escape routes; watch out for trees stumps if the snow cover is poor.
- *Route Discription* : from Plan de l'Aiguille head north, sidling round in a big arc to face Chamonix; negotiate as best you can the clearings, staying always on the left of the Blaitière torrent. Passing le Pré du Rocher (1600 m), pick up a track (below and left) leading back to the cable-car parking-space.

La Combe des Glaciers

Same characteristics as the Pré du Rocher (orientation: north-west).
- *Route Description*: from Plan de l'Aiguille head south under the cables of the top cable-car into the big bowl immediately beside the cable-car station. Stay in the bowl for around 500 vertical metres, but find, around 1850 m altitude, three big boulders on the left side of the gully. From the bottom-most boulder, look for a track leaving horizontally on the right. Follow it to the car park.

LA VALLEE BLANCHE

L a VALLEE BLANCHE permet à des skieurs moyens de voyager au cœur du plus vaste domaine glaciaire des Alpes françaises. Sa fréquentation pourrait laisser croire que son parcours est sans danger. Pourtant, de nombreux skieurs ont fait l'expérience ici d'une nuit sur glacier, pris au piège par l'obscurité ou le brouillard.

- **Difficulté** : Assez Difficile (en bonnes conditions); exige une bonne connaissance des glaciers.
- **Dénivellation** : 2800 m (2000 m jusqu'à la télécabine du Montenvers, s'il n'y a pas suffisamment de neige pour rejoindre Chamonix); distance 17 km; horaire: 2 à 5 h.
- **Engagement** : engagé. Pas de pistes sur ce versant.
- **Cheminement** : assez complexe.
- **Dangers** : crevasses, mauvais temps (orientation), altitude.
- **Période propice** : février à avril.
- **Matériel** : approprié au ski sur glacier.
- **Itinéraire** : descendre skis sur l'épaule l'arête de l'AIGUILLE DU MIDI, où de solides mains courantes sont installées. Chausser les skis sur un replat, puis, après un petit détour par le sud-est pour éviter des crevasses, gagner à droite le bassin supérieur de la VALLEE BLANCHE qui s'étale sous la face sud de l'aiguille. Rallier le col du Gros Rognon par une large boucle (3415 m). Descendre la belle combe qui passe au pied de la face nord-est du MONT-BLANC DU TACUL. Parvenu au bas de celle-ci, suivre la pente du glacier, et obliquer rive gauche de la BEDIAIRE, vers 3000 m (au niveau de la VIERGE). Se diriger en direction du PETIT ROGNON pour franchir une première zone de séracs. Toujours dans la même direction, traverser à flanc pour descendre au mieux un imposant chaos de séracs, en se dirigeant vers le refuge du REQUIN (2516 m). Quand le glacier se calme, revenir en son milieu sur le replat de la "Salle à Manger". Eviter les crevasses par la droite et descendre le long plat du GLACIER DU TACUL (jonction de deux glaciers TACUL et LESCHAUX). Skier dans sa partie centrale; franchir quelques crevasses pour descendre des pentes régulières en direction de gros rochers posés sur la glace. Eviter ensuite, par la gauche, une zone très crevassée, puis revenir dans la partie médiane du glacier. Vers 1650 m, quitter par la gauche la MER DE GLACE pour prendre le chemin ascendant des "Mottets". Terminer la descente par le chemin du MONTENVERS qui ramène aux téléskis des PLANARDS.

THE VALLEE BLANCHE

*L*a VALLEE BLANCHE allows skiers of only average ability to penetrate the bigges
glaciated region of the French Alps. Their numbers could let one think that this iti
nerary is without danger. However, more than one person has bivouacked here, a
night out on the glacier without being prepared, trapped by the darkness or the fog..

- *Technical Diff.* : Quite Difficult (in good conditions); demands a good
  knowledge of glaciated terrain.
- *Vertical Drop* : 2800 m (2000 m to the Montenvers gondola if the snow
  cover is insufficient to ski down to Chamonix); distance
  17 km; 2 - 5 hours.
- *Commitment* : quite serious. No marked runs here.
- *Route finding* : complex.
- *Dangers* : crevasses, bad weather (very difficult to find the route in
  poor visibility), altitude.
- *Suitable period* : february to april.
- *Equipment* : as for glacier skiing.
- *Route Description* : descend the arete of the AIGUILLE DU MIDI, carrying the
skis (fixed ropes in place). Put skis on where the ridge widens then, after a small
detour to the south-east to avoid some crevasses, gain the upper basin of the VAL-
LEE BLANCHE, passing under the south face of the Aiguille du Midi. Holding height as much as possible, pass through the Col du Gros Rognon (3415 m). A huge
bowl now opens up. Passing under the north-east flank of the MONT-BLANC du
TACUL, follow the fall-line of the glacier. Staying on the left side of the main glacial trough, negotiate the first crevassed zone in the direction of the PETIT
ROGNON. Still in the same direction, sidle around to descend at best an impo-
sing chaos of seracs and holes. When things calm down, either traverse left to the
Refuge du REQUIN (2516 m) or back towards the middle of the glacier, onto the
first big flat after the ice fall ("Salle à Manger"). Avoid a new barrier of crevasses
by tending right, descending the long gentle slopes issuing from the GLACIER DU
TACUL. At the junction with the LESCHAUX glacier, stay towards the middle,
negotiating a few crevasses (shallow) to arrive via gentle slopes beside a huge granite block resting on the ice. Another long schuss tending left to avoid a heavily
crevassed zone brings one opposite the "Pas de Chèvre". Rejoining the middle of
the glacier, negotiate a last broken passage. Towards 1650 m, quit the MER DE
GLACE on the left bank, by the track leading up to Les Mottets; from here, the
MONTENVERS track down through the forest to Les PLANARDS and Chamonix.

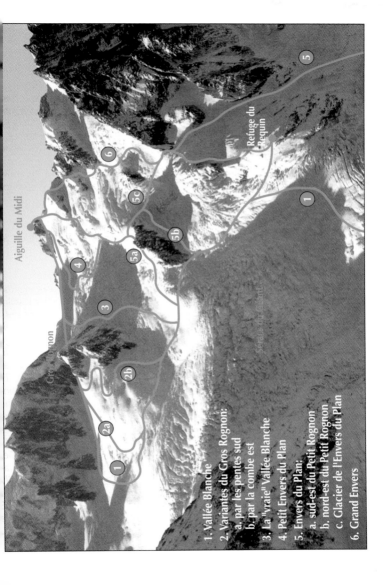

Aiguille du Midi

Gros Rognon

Refuge du Requin

1. Vallée Blanche
2. Variantes du Gros Rognon:
   a. par les pentes sud
   b. par la combe est
3. La "vraie" Vallée Blanche
4. Petit Envers du Plan
5. Envers du Plan:
   a. sud-est du Petit Rognon
   b. nord-est du Petit Rognon
   c. Glacier de l'Envers du Plan
6. Grand Envers

LES VARIANTES DE LA VALLEE BLANCHE

Variante du Gros Rognon (photo précédente)

Un vaste secteur où la neige reste souvent de bonne qualité. Pour les skieurs à la recherche de pentes plus soutenues que l'itinéraire classique.

- **Accès** : Téléphérique de l'Aiguille du Midi.
- **Dénivellation** : 600 m pour la variante.
- **Orientation** : sud-est.
- **Diff. technique** : Assez Difficile.
- **Engagement** : assez engagé.
- **Cheminement** : peu complexe par bonne visibilité.
- **Danger** : crevasses.
- **Matériel** : approprié au ski sur glacier.
- **Itinéraire** : au Col du Gros Rognon, skier sur le flanc ouest du Gros Rognon, puis revenir dès que possible à gauche, à l'aplomb des câbles de la télécabine de la Vallée Blanche. Deux options sont alors possibles:

  1 - Skier direction sud-ouest, de façon à revenir sur l'itinéraire classique. Attention aux crevasses, peu visibles, même par faible enneigement.

  2 - Pousuivre la traversée direction sud-est pour passer à proximité d'un éperon rocheux (3276 m). Descendre une vaste baie glaciaire et aborder une zone très crevassée, qu'on contourne généralement par la gauche. Rejoindre l'itinéraire classique par une succession de belles pentes entrecoupées de zone planes. Il est également possible, suivant l'état du glacier, de s'aventurer dans la belle combe Est. Pour cela, obliquer à gauche vers 3050 m.

THE VARIANTS OF THE VALLEE BLANCHE

Gros Rognon Variant (preceding photo)

This is a huge area where the snow often stays good for a long time. It is ideal for people looking for a more sustained run down.

- *Access*   : *"Aiguille du Midi" cablecar.*
- *Vertical Drop*   : *600 m.*
- *Orientation*   : *south-east.*
- *Technical Diff.*   : *quite difficult.*
- *Commitment*   : *quite serious.*
- *Route Finding*   : *not too bad in good visibility.*
- *Dangers*   : *crevasses.*
- *Equipment*   : *as for glacier skiing.*
- *Route Description* : *from the "Col du Gros Rognon" ski under the rocky west face of the "Gros Rognon", then go leftwards as soon as possible to reach a point directly below the cables of the gondola. From here you have a choice of two routes:*

  1 - *Ski in a south-westerly direction to reach the classic itinerary. Watch out for the crevasses which are often difficult to see.*

  2 - *Continue traversing south-east, passing close to a rocky spur (3276 m), and then head down into a huge glacial bowl. You come to a very crevassed zone which you generally turn on the left and then continue down to meet the classic itinerary by lovely rolling slopes. It is sometimes possible to ski left at 3050 m to join another bowl (the "Combe Est") although this depends on the state of the glacier.*

Variante de la vraie Vallée Blanche (photo précédente)

C'est l'itinéraire original de la Vallée Blanche, où la neige reste longtemps poudreuse. De grandes crevasses au départ du glacier rendent souvent impraticable cet itinéraire.

- **Accès**   : Téléphérique de l'Aiguille du Midi.
- **Dénivellation**   : 700 pour la variante.
- **Orientation**   : est.
- **Diff. technique** : Assez Difficile.
- **Engagement**   : engagé.
- **Cheminement**   : complexe.
- **Matériel**   : approprié au ski sur glacier.
- **Dangers**   : crevasses. Séracs.
- **Itinéraire** : suivre le départ normal de la VALLEE BLANCHE et venir à gauche en direction de la combe qui borde le versant nord du GROS ROGNON. Entrer dans celle-ci par un ressaut raide (main courante utile). Suivre la combe sous les séracs sur une centaine de mètres, pour vite la quitter par la gauche. Une succession de belles pentes permettent de rejoindre, de façon évidente, la Vallée Blanche classique.

The real Vallée Blanche (preceding photo)

*L*arge crevasses often bar access to this valley, making the route impossible. Unfortunate really, because powder lasts a long time here.

- *Access*   : "Aiguille du Midi" cablecar.
- *Vertical Drop*   : 700 m for this variant.
- *Orientation*   : east.
- *Technical Diff.*   : quite difficult.
- *Commitment*   : serious.
- *Route Finding*   : complex.
- *Dangers*   : crevasses / séracs.
- *Equipment*   : as for glacier skiing.
- *Route Description* : attack as for the "classic" VALLEE BLANCHE but turn left into the bowl situated directly under the north face of the GROS ROGNON (steep passage, rope useful). Stay in the gully menaced by the seracs for about 100 m, then tend further left. A series of gentle rolls (attention crevasses!) lead in an obvious way to the junction with the "classic" VALLEE BLANCHE.

SECTEUR ENVERS DU PLAN

Situé sur le versant est-sud-est de l'arête Midi Plan, ces itinéraires audacieux, tracés au cœur d'un labyrinthe de glaciers cumulent toutes les difficultés du ski de haute montagne: complexité de l'itinéraire, pentes soutenues et engagement.

Le Petit Envers

Ce parcours moins fréquenté offre une alternative intéressante à la classique Vallée Blanche. Les pentes y sont un peu plus soutenues et le cheminement louvoie entre de spectaculaires zones de séracs.

- **Accès**   : Téléphérique de l'Aiguille du Midi.
- **Dénivellation** : 800 m.
- **Orientation**   : est-nord-est.
- **Diff. technique** : Assez Difficile.
- **Engagement**   : engagé.
- **Cheminement**   : peu complexe si la visibilité est bonne.
- **Matériel**   : approprié au ski sur glacier.
- **Danger**   : crevasses. Bon enneigement indispensable.
- **Itinéraire** : du bas de l'arête de l'Aiguille du Midi, se diriger à l'est pour aborder de façon évidente la belle pente située à gauche d'une petite arête neigeuse (point coté 3550). Au bas de celle-ci, on rejoint une zone plane sur le Glacier de la Vallée Blanche.

  Poursuivre direction nord-est par une pente douce, puis aborder une zone très crevassée que l'on franchit au mieux par des ponts de neiges. Continuer ensuite la traversée direction nord-est (ne pas descendre à droite), pour rejoindre un large plateau (3150 m). Partir alors direction Est pour gagner le col à l'amont du Petit Rognon (3005 m). Poursuivre par les différentes variantes de l'Envers du Plan qui sont décrites plus loin.

ENVERS DU PLAN SECTOR

*T*hese slopes are in a wild setting on the south-east side of the Midi-Plan arete. They take tortuous routes through a labyrinth of crevasses, and the skier or boarder who goes there must be prepared to deal with complex route finding, sustained slopes and a high degree of commitment.

Le Petit Envers

This itinerary can offer a good alternative to the classic "Vallée Blanche" on a busy day, although the slopes are a bit more sustained, and it can be difficult to find your way through the maze of crevasses and seracs.

- *Access* : "Aiguille du Midi" cablecar.
- *Vertical Drop* : 800 m for this variant.
- *Orientation* : east-north-east.
- *Technical Diff.* : quite difficult.
- *Commitment* : serious.
- *Route Finding* : not too bad in good visibility.
- *Dangers* : crevasses, good snow cover is required.
- *Equipment* : as for glacier skiing.
- *Route Description* : *from the bottom of the ridge coming down from the "Aiguille du Midi", head eastwards and ski the nice slope to the left of the little snowy ridge (spotheight 3550 m on the map). At the bottom of this slope you reach a flat area on the "Vallée Blanche" glacier. Go in a north-easterly direction down a gentle slope until you come to a very crevassed zone. Cross this as best you can using the snowbridges, and then continue traversing north-east (don't go down rightwards) to a large flat area at 3150 m. From here head east to reach the col above the "Petit Rognon" rock butress. Continue down by any of the "Envers du Plan" variations described below.*

L'Envers du Plan

Près de 1400 m de descente au cœur d'un système glaciaire complexe. Un itinéraire exceptionnel.

- **Accès**   : Téléphérique de l'Aiguille du Midi.
- **Dénivellation** : 1400 m jusqu'à la Mer de Glace.
- **Orientation**   : est.
- **Diff. technique** : Difficile.
- **Engagement**   : engagé.
- **Cheminement**   : complexe.
- **Matériel**   : approprié au ski sur glacier.
- **Dangers**   : risque d'avalanche après chaque épisode neigeux; dévissage sur neige dure; crevasses.
- **Itinéraire** : du bas de l'arête de l'Aiguille du Midi, partir à l'est, en longeant l'arête MIDI-PLAN. Quand celle-ci remonte, obliquer à droite vers un large replat. Le traverser au nord-est pour franchir une épaule (3420 m), donnant sur la combe issue du Col du Plan (courte pente à 40°/45°, rimaye). Prendre ensuite la combe à droite dominée un court instant par des séracs, puis tirer à gauche. Une pente plus soutenue amène à un plateau glaciaire (3150 m). Le traverser direction Est, franchir une zone crevassée, et gagner un petit col à l'amont du Petit Rognon (3005 m). Trois options sont alors possibles:

a) Par le versant sud-est du Petit Rognon: pente à 30°/35°, à skier seulement en neige de printemps. Rejoint l'itinéraire de la Vallée Blanche au niveau de la Bédière.

b) Par la combe nord-est du Petit Rognon: l'itinéraire le plus sûr en cas de mauvaises conditions de neige. Du col, faire un large détour par le nord afin de contourner une zone crevassée et revenir dans la combe bordant les rochers. La suivre de façon évidente et rejoindre l'itinéraire classique de la Vallée Blanche après une dernière pente raide.

c) Par le Glacier de l'Envers du Plan: cette option est l'itinéraire original. Du col, effectuer une longue traversée à flanc, direction nord, afin de passer en aval d'un éperon rocheux. Traverser le glacier de l'Envers du Plan, toujours au nord, jusqu'à la base de l'arête rocheuse du "Chapeau à Corne" (Aiguille du Requin).

Descendre le long des séracs, et, quand la pente devient plus raide, choisir entre deux solutions:

1 - Poursuivre tout droit, franchir un ressaut très raide - 40°, (dalles de granit sous-jacente) - et entrer dans un couloir un peu moins pentu. On rejoint ainsi un des couloirs de sortie qui amènent à la Mer de Glace (ceux les plus à droites sont les plus raides: 35°).

2 - Traverser à droite et descendre une pente très soutenue (35°). Ensuite, comme précédemment, emprunter un des couloirs de sortie.

Conseils: cette portion finale de l'Envers du plan est particulièrement dangereuse en neige dure (dévissage). Plus qu'ailleurs une corde peut être utile pour assurer un compagnon un peu timide dans ses virages.

Les risque d'avalanche y sont toujours importants après chaque chute de neige.

L'Envers du Plan

A fantastic descent, with almost 1400 m of vertical drop through a complex glacial system.

- *Access* : "Aiguille du Midi" cablecar.
- *Vertical Drop* : 1400 m to the "Mer de Glace".
- *Orientation* : east.
- *Technical Diff.* : difficult.
- *Commitment* : serious.
- *Route Finding* : complex.
- *Dangers* : avalanche prone after snowfall; risk of slipping and falling on hard snow; crevasses.
- *Equipment* : as for glacier skiing.
- *Route Description* : from the bottom of the ridge coming off the "Aiguille du Midi", traverse east alongside the "Midi-Plan arête". From where this ridge starts to go up, head down right to a flat area which you traverse in a north-easterly direction to reach a shoulder. Cross this and ski the short, steep (40°/45°) slope on the other side, to drop into the bowl which comes down from

the "Col du Plan". There is a large bergschrund (crevasse) at the bottom of this slope - beware! Now ski down rightwards into another bowl (séracs above) and then back left to follow a sustained slope down to a flat area (3150 m). Cross it, heading east, and then go down through a crevassed zone to reach the col above the "Petit Rognon" rock buttress. You now have a choice of three routes:

a) By the south-east side of the "Petit Rognon": 30° - 35° slope. Should only be done in spring snow conditions. This route joins up with the classic "Vallée Blanche" itinerary at "la Bédière".

b) By the north-east bowl of the "Petit Rognon": the safest way down if the snow is bad. From the col head north to avoid a crevassed area, and then come back round to drop into the bowl bordered on its right by a rock wall. Follow it down (obvious) and, after a final steep slope, meet up with the classic "Vallée Blanche" itinerary.

c) By the "Envers du Plan" glacier: the original route down. From the col make a long traverse north and pass below a rocky spur. Cross the "Envers du Plan" glacier (still heading north) to reach the base of the "Chapeau à Corne" ridge which comes off the "Aiguille du Requin". Ski down alongside the séracs until the slope steepens and then either:

   1 - Go straight down the slope, negotiating one very steep section (40°; snow lying on steep, granite slabs), to reach a gully which is slightly less steep. Follow this down towards the exit couloirs which take you out onto the "Mer de Glace" (the couloirs get progressively easier from right to left. The right-hand one is at 35°). Or:

   2 - Traverse rightwards and ski a very sustained slope (35°) to join the route described above.

Safety Tip: this last section of the "Envers du Plan" itinerary is particularly dangerous when the snow is hard. Don't hesitate to get the rope out of the sack. These slopes are avalanche prone after fresh snow.

Le Grand Envers

La plus difficile et la plus spectaculaire des descentes du secteur de l'Envers du Plan.

- **Accès** : Téléphérique de l'Aiguille du Midi.
- **Dénivellation** : 1400 m jusqu'à la Mer de Glace.
- **Orientation** : nord-est.
- **Diff. technique** : Très Difficile.
- **Engagement** : engagé.
- **Cheminement** : complexe.
- **Matériel** : approprié au ski sur glacier.
- **Dangers** : risque d'avalanche après chaque épisode neigeux; dévissage sur neige dure; crevasses.

Itinéraire : de l'Aiguille du Midi, skier, au nord, en direction de l'arête Midi Plan. Atteindre une antécime (point côté 3626 m) en 10 mn de montée (en escalier). Longer le versant sud-ouest (pente raide) jusqu'à une épaule neigeuse. On aborde ainsi un premier mur (150 m à 40°) que l'on traversera d'abord pour le descendre à gauche.

La rimaye franchie, traverser à gauche, en aval du Col du Plan, en direction de rochers. Descendre une épaule, puis traverser à gauche pour aborder une seconde pente raide (100 m, 40°). Franchir la rimaye, traverser et descendre d'abord en rive gauche du glacier, puis, après une zone crevassée revenir à droite en direction d'un replat pour repérer des rochers émergeant du glacier (3061 m). De ces rochers, traverser de nouveau à gauche pour contourner de larges crevasses. Une dernière pente, et l'on retrouve l'itinéraire de l'Envers du Plan sous l'arête du Chapeau à Corne.

Le Grand Envers

*T**he most difficult and the most spectacular of these descents.*

- *Access*   : *"Aiguille du Midi" cablecar.*
- *Vertical Drop*   : *1400 m to the "Mer de Glace".*
- *Orientation*   : *north-east.*
- *Technical Diff.*   : *very difficult.*
- *Commitment*   : *serious.*
- *Route Finding*   : *complex.*
- *Dangers*   : *avalanche prone after snowfall; risk of slipping and falling on hard snow; crevasses.*
- *Equipment*   : *as for glacier skiing.*
- *Route Description* : *from the "Aiguille du Midi" ski north towards the "Midi Plan arête". Climb up this arete to a small summit (10 mins. of side-stepping spotheight 3626 m). Follow the steep, south-west (right) side of the ridge to a snowy shoulder. Drop down left into the obvious bowl, which you traverse to ski down its left-hand-side (150 m at 40°). Once across the bergschrund (crevasse), traverse left under the "Col du Plan" towards some rocks. Go down a shoulder and then traverse left to another steep slope. Ski this (100 m at 40°), cross the bergschrund at the bottom and then traverse to reach the left bank of the glacier. Descend past a crevassed zone, and then come back right towards a flat area, from where you can see some rocks sticking out of the glacier (3061 m). From these rocks traverse left again to avoid some big crevasses, and then head down one last steep slope to reach the "Envers du Plan" route at the base of the "Chapeau à Corne" ridge.*

SECTEUR HELBRONNER

e versant sud du massif du Mont-Blanc, desservi par le téléphérique de la point Helbronner (3462 m) nous offre, avec le glacier de Toule, un site xceptionnel. "L'envers" du Mont-Blanc et son immense arête de Peuterey sont ncore plus impressionnants que le versant français.
' accès au Glacier de Toule reste réservé aux bons skieurs sportifs puisque, vant de chausser les skis, il faudra d'abord rejoindre le Col de Toule, et desendre des escaliers vertigineux (compter 30 minutes d'effort).
Un inconvénient, associé au faible débit du téléphérique, qui fait que ce sec-eur est relativement peu fréquenté.

Accès : **En voiture** : rejoindre Entrèves (18 km de Chamonix), situé à1 km
après la sortie du tunnel du Mont-Blanc.
Bus   : départ quotidien pour Courmayeur en début de matinée
(à la gare SNCF de Chamonix).
En cas de fermeture du tunnel:
- Rejoindre Entrèves par le Col des Montets, le Col de la Forclaz et le Col du Grand Saint-Bernard (200 km...).
- En téléphérique, via l'Aiguille du Midi et la Télécabine de la Vallée Blanche (ne fonctionne en général qu'à partir de la fin du mois de mars).
- En ski de randonnée: 250 m de montée depuis la Vallée Blanche (cf. "Mont-Blanc, ski de randonnée", éditions Vamos).

Forfaits   : à la montée ou à la journée (à peine plus cher). Le Téléphérique de la Pointe Helbronner n'est inclus dans aucun ski pass.
Restaurant : sympathique restaurant à Pavillon (station intermédiaire).
Tél. utiles : Office du Tourisme de Courmayeur: (00 39) 0165 84 66 58.
Funivia de Monte Bianco (téléphérique): (00 39) 0165 89 925.
Bureau des Guides de Courmayeur: (00 39) 0165 84 20 64 ou (00 39) 0165 84 23 57.
Secours en Montagne: 0165 23 82 22.

Couverture téléphonique
: assez bonne couverture sur le versant italien.

HELBRONNER SECTOR

*T*he Italian side of these mountains, accessed from the Helbronner cablec. (3462 m), is perhaps even more spectacular than the French side. Th south-facing Toule glacier offers a fantastic run down, under the summits of Mont Blanc's impressive Peuterey Ridge.

The following route is only suitable for reasonably fit, good skiers; before sta. ting the descent you first have to reach the "Col de Toule" and then go dow the steep stairs to get onto the glacier (approx. 30 mins. of effort). With a archaic cablecar and snow conditions which are rarely very good, you soo start to realize why this area sees relatively little traffic.

- *Access* : **By car** : go to Entrèves by the Mont Blanc tunnel (1 km from th tunnel exit / 18 km from Chamonix).

  By bus : daily service from the main train station in Chamonix. Tak the Courmayeur bus which leaves early in the morning.

  If the tunnel is closed you can get to Entrèves by going throug Switzerland and over the "Col du Grand Saint-Bernard" (200 km fror Chamonix).

  By cablecar: A gondola links the summit of the "Aiguille du Midi" t "Helbronner", but it only starts running at the end of March.

  On skis: from the classic "Vallée Blanche" itinerary you can reach th "Col de Toule" by a 250 m climb. Ski-touring equipment is require (touring bindings and skins). You can find a description of this route i the "Mont Blanc Ski Tours" guidebook (also published by Vamos).

- *Ski Pass* : the Helbronner cablecar is not included in any ski pass. Buy single ticket or a day pass (not much more expensive).
- *Restaurant* : you'll find a nice restaurant at "Pavillon" (the mid-station).

- *Useful Telephone Numbers* (mobile phones work well on the Italian side): Courmayeur Tourist Office: (+39) 0165 846658 "Funivia de Monte Bianco" (cablecar): (+39) 0165 89925 "Courmayeur Guides" Office: (+39) 0165 842064 or (+39) 0165 842357 Mountain Rescue: 0165 238222

Le Glacier de Toule

Un bel itinéraire de grande envergure qui offre au skieur exigeant de grands espaces peu parcourus. A savourer de préférence au printemps, quand la neige dégèle en surface. L'enchaînement Glacier de Toule / Combe de la Vierge / Vallée Blanche est une combinaison idéale pour remplir une bonne journée de ski.

Accès	: Téléphérique d'Helbronner à Entrèves (Italie), ou Aiguille du Midi + Télécabine d'Helbronner, ou en peaux de phoque depuis la VALLEE BLANCHE.
Orientation	: sud.
Dénivelée	: 1237 m jusqu'à la station intermédiaire de PAVILLON.
Difficulté	: Difficile; exige une bonne connaissance des glaciers.
Engagement	: engagé.
Dangers	: crevasses; pente soutenue.
Cheminement	: assez complexe.
Période proprice	: janvier à avril (partir tôt, la neige est très travaillée par le soleil).

Itinéraire : de la pointe HELBRONNER, rejoindre le Col des FLAMBEAUX, et traverser à flanc, versant nord, sous le GRAND FLAMBEAU. Gagner le Col Occidental de TOULE, puis descendre l'escalier qui conduit au glacier. Après les cent premiers mètres pentus, on skie dans une large combe. Une boucle à gauche permet d'éviter des pentes plus raides. Elle conduit à une cuvette neigeuse. Venir alors vers les rochers pour contourner une large crevasse; puis longer les faces rocheuses pour quitter par la gauche le glacier. Traverser à l'est une succession de grandes moraines qui ramènent à l'aplomb de PAVILLON, la station intermédiaire.

Variantes: Deux variantes parcourent le Glacier de Toule, avec chacune un passage raide (35°).
- Par la rive droite: descendre en tirant le plus tôt possible à droite pour venir traverser le large plateau le plus haut possible. Continuer à proximité de rochers pour aborder une pente soutenue. Toujours le long des rochers,

venir dépasser la base d'un éperon rocheux, puis revenir, toujours à gauche en direction de Pavillon.
- Par le Glacier d'Entrèves: descendre en tirant le plus tôt possible à droite. Longer les rochers et venir à l'aplomb d'une brèche, que l'on atteint à pied. rechausser et descendre en tirant à droite. Venir ainsi sur le Glacier d'Entrèves. Une fois la base d'un éperon dépassée, revenir à gauche par une longue traversée en direction de Pavillon.

Descente sur La Palud:
De Pavillon, descendre les pentes qui partent à gauche. En amont des pare avalanches, passer à droite, sous les câbles, pour rejoindre une crête. L suivre pour revenir à gauche par un long schuss. Descendre alors une bell pente parsemée de mélèzes, puis suivre un couloir de plus en plus étroit. L suite est évidente jusqu'à La Palud.

Glacier de Toule

*T*his is the place to go to find wide, open spaces, far from the crowds. Bes savoured in sexy, spring snow conditions when the searing sun slightly sof tens the surface of the snow (sorry about that - translating can get pretty tedious at times). The descent of the Toule Glacier combined with the Combe de l. Vierge on the french side constitutes almost a perfect day's skiing.

- Access	: Helbronner cable-car at Entrèves, ITALY - Aiguille d Midi and the Vallée Blanche gondola - On skins from the Vallée Blanche.
- Aspect	: south.
- Vertical Drop	: 1237 m until the PAVILLON mid-station.
- Technical Diff.	: Difficult; demands a good knowledge of glaciated ter rain.
- Commitment	: serious.
- Dangers	: crevasses, sustained slopes.

Pavillon

Pointe Helbronner

1. Glacier de Toule
2. Glacier de Toule, rive droite
3. Glacier d'Entrèves

- *Route finding*   : quite complex.
- *Suitable Period*   : january-april (leave early, south facing slopes).
- *Route Description*: from Pointe HELBRONNER, reach the Col des FLAM-
BEAUX and traverse under the GRAND FLAMBEAU to the staircase leading
down the italian side. Ski down keeping the rocks on the left. Arriving hard
up against a granite wall, take the couloir between the rocks and the seracs
on the right (steep). Continue down the final glacial tongue then traverse left
over a series of moraine walls, which brings one directly above the PAVIL-
LON midstation.

Variations:
There are 2 variations possible on this descent; both have steep (35°) sections.
- By the right bank of the glacier: As soon as you can, traverse rightwards and
cross a large flat area as high as possible. Head down close to the rocks to
reach a sustained slope. Stay close to these rocks until below the base of the
spur, and then head left. Continue leftwards to the mid-station (Pavillon).
- By the Entrèves Glacier: As soon as you can, traverse rightwards towards the
rocks. Follow these down until you arrive directly beneath a notch in the
ridge. Climb up to this notch on foot, get your skis back on, and descend
rightwards towards the "Entrèves" Glacier. Once past the base of the spur,
turn left and head back to "Pavillon" by a series of long, leftward traverses.

Descent to La Palud (bottom station):
From "Pavillon" go down the slopes on the left. From above the avalanche
barriers cross right under the cables to reach a rise. Follow this and then head
straight down leftwards towards the larch trees. Ski down the lovely, sparsely
wooded slopes to enter a couloir which gets progressively narrower. The rest
of the descent down to La Palud is obvious.

Combe de la Vierge

Cet itinéraire est le départ de la version italienne de la VALLEE BLANCHE.

- **Accès**   : POINTE HELBRONNER.
- **Orientation**   : nord.
- **Dénivelée**   : 400 m pour rejoindre la VALLEE BLANCHE.
- **Difficulté**   : Assez Difficile; exige une bonne connaissance des gla-
                       ciers.
- **Engagement**   : assez engagé.
- **Dangers**   : crevasses.
- **Cheminement**   : assez simple.
- **Itinéraire** : du COL DES FLAMBEAUX, prendre nord-est en passant à proximité du téléski, puis descendre dans la combe. Contourner par la droite une large crevasse et gagner par des pentes régulières l'itinéraire normal de la VALLEE BLANCHE.

La Combe de la Noire

Variante très engagée, qui consiste à passer rive droite des séracs du GEANT.

- **Accès**   : Pointe HELBRONNER.
- **Orientation**   : nord.
- **Dénivelée**   : 1000 m jusqu'à la Salle-à-Manger.
- **Difficulté**   : Très Difficile; pour skieurs-alpinistes.
- **Engagement**   : très engagé.
- **Dangers**   : crevasses, dévissage, avalanche.
- **Cheminement**   : très complexe. Demande de très bonnes conditions
                       d'enneigement.
- **Itinéraire** : du Col des FLAMBEAUX, partir à l'Est en direction de l'Aiguille MARBREE. De sa base, remonter à pied une centaine de mètres pour gagner un replat. Là, toujours dans la même direction, traverser un long plateau pour rallier le bord droit du glacier. Descendre des pentes de plus en plus soutenues, entrecoupées de crevasses. Parvenu au niveau des séracs du GEANT, se tenir au plus près des rochers, en cherchant au mieux son chemin dans le dédale des crevasses, pour sortir à la Salle-à-Manger.

La Combe de la Vierge

*I*talian version of the VALLEE BLANCHE.

- *Access*   : POINTE HELBRONNER.
- *Aspect*   : north.
- *Vertical Drop*   : 400 m into the VALLEE BLANCHE.
- *Technical Diff.*   : Quite Difficult; demands a good knowledge of glaciated terrain.
- *Engagement*   : quite serious.
- *Dangers*   : crevasses.
- *Route-finding*   : quite simple.
- *Route Description*: from the COL DES FLAMBEAUX, head north-east passing close by the T-bar; then drop into a wide bowl. Turn on the right a big crevasse and reach by gentle slopes the "classic" VALLEE BLANCHE.

La Combe de la Noire

*V*ery serious variant, passing on the right bank of the Vallée Blanche icefall.

- *Access*   : Pointe HELBRONNER.
- *Aspect*   : north.
- *Vertical Drop*   : 1000 m until the Salle-à-Manger.
- *Engagement*   : very serious.
- *Technical Diff.*   : Very Difficult; for ski-mountaineers.
- *Dangers*   : crevasses, slipping, avalanches.
- *Route-finding*   : very complex, needing good snow cover.
- *Route Description*: from the Col des FLAMBEAUX, head east towards the Aiguille MARBREE. From it's base, climb up on foot 100 m to reach a flat. Once there, continue in the same direction, traversing a long plateau until one arrives on the right bank of the glacier. Ski down slopes which become steeper, and cut by crevasses. At the level of the GEANT seracs, stay close to the rocks on the right, searching, as best one can from above, the best solution through the maze to exit onto the Salle-à-Manger.

Pointe Helbronner

1. Combe de la Vierge
2. Combe de la Noire

LES HOUCHES

Agréablement située dans la forêt, la station des Houches offre aussi un beau hors-piste de proximité, qui peut s'envisager lorsque la visibilité n'est pas très bonne (grâce aux arbres qui constituent des repères pour évaluer la pente). Il faut suffisamment de neige toutefois pour ne pas risquer d'abîmer de jeunes arbres. Signalons en particulier la forêt qui cerne la piste des Plancerts. Côté "grand hors-pistes" on trouve, au départ de la télécabine du Prarion, la Combe du Prarion, superbe descente par un bon enneigement.

La Combe du Prarion

- **Orientation**   : nord.
- **Dénivelée**   : 928 m; de 1967 m à 1039 m.
- **Difficulté**   : Assez Difficile.
- **Engagement**   : assez engagé.
- **Cheminement**   : simple dans la moitié supérieure, puis plus complexe.
- **Danger**   : risques d'avalanche de poudreuse en début d'hiver, de neige lourde au printemps (le sol est composé d'herbes couchées et de rhododendrons).
- **Itinéraire** : depuis le haut de la télécabine du Prarion (1853 m) gagner la Tête du Prarion (1967 m): 15 à 20 mn de marche, skis sur l'épaule. 50 mètres avant le sommet, plonger à droite - souvent petite corniche - dans une large combe orientée vers les Houches. Se laisser aller d'une contrepente à l'autre, puis suivre les vallonnements entrecoupés de petits ressauts. Quand les "broussailles" se font de plus en plus denses, traverser largement à droite pour suivre les pylônes de la télécabine jusqu'en bas.

(Rp. Jean-Pierre MANSART)

LES HOUCHES

*P*leasant station in the forest, Les Houches also offers fine off-piste close to the lifts, worth the visit when visibility is low (thanks to the trees). Enough snow is needed so as not to destroy the young trees. We mention particularly the forest around the piste des Plancerts.

The major off-piste run is the Combe du Prarion, a superb descent with good snow-cover.

La Combe du Prarion

- *Aspect*   : north.
- *Vertical Drop*   : 928 m; from 1967 m to 1039 m.
- *Technical Diff.* : Quite Difficult.
- *Engagement*   : quite serious.
- *Route-finding*   : easy in the top-half, then more complex.
- *Danger*   : avalanche risk early in winter and of heavy snow in spring (ground cover consists of flattened grass and rhododendrons).
- *Route Description* : from the Prarion gondola (1853 m) climb on foot to the Tête du Prarion (1967 m): 15-20 mn. 50 metres before the summit plunge right into a wide gully facing Les Houches. Use the gully walls, then follow the rolls. When the going gets tough because of the vegetation, traverse right until under the gondola pylons.

1ère partie:
vers une pratique responsable du ski hors-pistes

2ème partie:
le plus beau domaine du monde...

Table of contents

Part one:
Responsible off-piste practice

Part two:
The finest domaine in the world

REALLY

DAFT

IDEAS

HUNTING
OUTFIT

A MODEL OF DESIRED
PREY IS AFFIXED TO A
HAT →

D. I. SASTER

summersdale

REALLY DAFT IDEAS

Summersdale Publishers Ltd
46 West Street
Chichester
West Sussex
PO19 1RP
UK

www.summersdale.com

Printed and bound in Great Britain

ISBN 1 84024 461 5

REALLY
DAFT
IDEAS

CONTENTS

REALLY

DAFT

INVENTIONS

Ever wondered what the little thing on the end of your shoelace is called? Probably not. But at one point in time, it didn't exist. Someone had to invent it: they had an idea, turned it into a reality and voilà! The aglet became a major part of our lives. We've all dreamed about one day discovering our own special invention and living off the profits of our genius, and it is said that everybody has one good idea in them that just needs to be brought to the surface. Yet for these inventors, it probably would have been a better idea to just stay in bed.

The body

A US INVENTOR believed that sniffing particular combinations of odours could help increase the blood flow to certain parts of the male body, thus proving to be an alternative to Viagra™. He created odours which could be administered by scented cloths, sprays or scratch-and-sniff patches. Sadly his scent combinations – including lavender/pumpkin pie and doughnut/liquorice – didn't really do the trick.

NOT TO BE outdone, the French came up with the ultimate in safe sex. Using a whole body suit made from a transparent plastic with an attached condom, you would be protected against all sexually transmitted diseases. The protection worked a little too well, however: it seems not many were keen to have sex with someone in a plastic bag.

REALLY DAFT INVENTIONS

A BARMY COMMUTER in Tokyo caused chaos on a crowded tube train one morning when his rubber underpants unexpectedly inflated to thirty times their original size. He had designed them himself as an automatic means of protection from drowning in the event of a tidal wave, but when they accidentally self-activated on the train they began to suffocate his fellow commuters. They were only saved by the quick thinking of one passenger who managed to burst the underpants with a pencil.

A 'CONTOURED ULTERIOR Pouch', or CUP, designed to fit over a man's private parts, was concocted in the US. The inventor claimed that this would boost a man's ego by drawing envious glances from all he passes.

A BRITISH INVENTOR came up with the idea of a fart collecting device. A collecting tube runs from the subject's behind into a bag where the specially brewed odours can gather. These can then be released when the time is right. Apparently the time for this particular invention was never right.

REALLY DAFT INVENTIONS

A NEW YORK man formulated a new exercise regime based around tug of war. Two plates connected by an elastic cord form the basis of this exercise. Two participants grip a plate between their teeth and then simply pull in an attempt to dislodge the plate from the opponent's mouth. This exertion is intended to strengthen the jaw and neck muscles.

A RIVAL INVENTOR claimed to have found a way to help you exercise the correct muscles for neck toning; muscles which are normally only worked when you chew, smile, grimace or talk. The Chin Pump works by piston power. You place your chin in the chin cup and proceed to move your jaw up and down. The piston's resistance helps work your hyoid to tone your infrahyoid.

IN THE US a urinal was designed with the intention of encouraging more accurate aim. An entertainment system with TV would be activated only when the sensors in the receptacle sensed the pressure and temperature of the urine stream. Another kind of peer pressure for the urinal.

REALLY DAFT INVENTIONS

A CALIFORNIA MAN devised a way to entertain the unborn. His contraption included a strap to secure a personal stereo and speakers to the abdomen of an expectant mother, allowing music to be played for the enjoyment of the foetus at any time of day. The inventor suggested that this would make for a happier baby.

ANOTHER AMERICAN INVENTION, this time to make the process of labour slightly less drawn out, required the heavily pregnant woman to be strapped down to a table. This was then spun at great speed and used centrifugal force to encourage the baby to emerge.

US scientists came up with the idea of a wig-flipping device. This invention comprised a spring-loaded wig which is worn in the normal way. The difference being that it can be activated by the wearer in order to surprise and amuse friends or baffle foes.

Animals

THE GERMANS CREATED a device for looking after the toilet habits of your canine friend. It comprises a plastic tube with two open ends. One end is connected to an all-purpose suction unit, while the other has a funnel attached to the dog's behind. The device prevents the soiling of parks and play areas... and can also be used on humans.

AN AMERICAN MAN who was also concerned about dogs soiling the streets was daft enough to use satellite-tracking devices to locate the offending deposits. In an attempt to persuade city leaders to ban dogs from his neighbourhood, he used a global positioning system not for stopping drug smugglers or pinpointing military, targets but for charting dog droppings.

IN ORDER TO make mutt mealtimes less messy, one dog owner came up with the idea of a strap to restrict the movement of a dog's ears while eating. Especially useful for breeds such as basset hounds and cocker spaniels, the strap is used to tie back the ears to prevent them getting in the way of the food.

A Yorkshire man, evidently an animal lover, invented a ladder to enable spiders to climb out of a bath. The arachnid emergency exit comprises a thin, flexible rubber strip which follows the inner contours of the bath and is attached to the rim using a suction pad.

MEANWHILE, A LEASH for imaginary pets was designed by another British man, who wanted a pet he could take for walkies without the hassle of cleaning and feeding a real-life animal. The leash is rigid and supports a harness and collar. A micro loudspeaker in the collar connects to a control circuit in the handle to produce a variety of barks and growls.

GRRR

A TUBE THAT runs round your clothing can be used to keep your pet hamster or guinea pig busy as you go about your day. Keep him entertained with images of his natural habitat on your clothes and the inventor claims you will have one happy pet.

Habits

AN ASHTRAY WHICH sends out a warning signal was invented in the US to aid people trying to quit smoking. An alarm is triggered every time you reach for your smoke. But what happens when you throw the ashtray out the window?

IN THE US one man invented a device to encourage teenagers to keep their teeth braces on. The patient's mouth is fitted with a magnetically controlled alarm that makes an irritating sound until the brace is in place, at which point a magnet on the brace deactivates the alarm. The designer's theory was that the sound of the alarm would be more embarrassing than actually wearing the brace.

IN 1882 ONE inventor found a novel way to wake people from their slumber. By suspending a light object above the head of the sleeper one could set a trigger that would cause the object to fall at any given time. This would wake the person and get them off to a brand new day. Thankfully, someone else invented the alarm clock.

REALLY DAFT INVENTIONS

A SOUND MUFFLER for the purpose of absorbing shouts was invented in the US. By screaming into it, the noise and thus the disturbance of others is reduced. Coated in foam, the muffler has a light meter that shows the intensity of any outburst. It was thought that this could be an aid for anger management, but sales never took off and it was – quietly – shelved. Proving that when we shout, we want to be heard.

Transport

IN THE EARLY 1900s a German designed a train system that he claimed would solve the eternal problem of delays on the railways. Large trains would have a gap in the centre allowing smaller trains to pass through, thereby avoiding any hold-ups.

A HORSE-POWERED MINIBUS was devised in the UK. The horse walks along a treadmill in the middle of the bus and powers the wheels via a gearbox. A thermometer under the horse's collar is connected to the vehicle instrument panel so the driver can cool down the horse using a handle with a damp mop on the end.

A WELL-KNOWN TECHNOLOGY company came up with the idea of allocating toilet reservation tickets on commercial airliners. Reservations were based on class and price of ticket. Those in the cheapest seats would have to wait until everyone else had relieved themselves before they could get to the toilet.

In the 1960s, someone had the notion to build a gasoline motor into a pogo stick that would be sparked off each time the stick hit the ground. The motor then powered the stick higher and higher into the air, but sadly it did not include any safety features. An invention, some might say, that hit new heights of stupidity.

REALLY DAFT INVENTIONS

AN INVENTION INTENDED to restore traditional British courtesy is a car registration plate that indicates the sex of the driver. Though, as we know, the road to hell is paved with good intentions. The plate has two sides of different colours, one for men and one for women, and so can be reversed easily for those who share a car with the opposite sex. The inventor's daft reasoning was that making the driver's sex immediately apparent would encourage other road users to be more polite.

Recreation

A HUNTING INVENTION comprised a long cloak that covered the whole body of the hunter and a hat with a model of the prey on it. The inventor envisaged dual benefits: firstly the hunter is hidden; and secondly the prey is drawn into the area. Of course, the cunning outfit might also turn the hunter into a target for other hunters.

ARE YOU EASILY tired? An American man invented a portable seat which can be worn on a waist-belt. The seat cushion pivots between a stowed position and a seating position so whenever the wearer needs a rest they can conveniently take a seat.

AN UMBRELLA WAS invented with the specific purpose of protecting drinks from the warming rays of the sun. The 'beerbrella' clips to the drinker's head and serves to maintain an area of shade around the drink at all times, thus keeping it suitably cool.

A NEW YORK man came up with the idea of a trumpet that could blow more than just notes – it would emit a flame from the bell of the trumpet, ignited by pressing the keys. The inventor, sadly, could not offer any practical application for his design.

HAD ENOUGH OF conventional sun shades? A floating helium-filled sun shade can be inflated and anchored in place using cables and weights in order to create shade on a sunny day. The designer claimed that the shade is more convenient than other types because it can easily be transported and inflated when needed.

A GOLF-LOVING AMERICAN invented an underwater golf swing training device. The golfer can adjust the resistance against the swing. The hydrodynamic paddle allows the golfer to practise a range of shots. The inventor asserted that this improves a player's game no end by increasing muscle strength.

Food

A PIONEERING NEW York chef designed a pizza mould that creates a series of concentric crusts covering almost the whole of a pizza. Toppings can then be squeezed in the tiny gaps between crusts. Would you like extra crusts with that?

REALLY DAFT INVENTIONS

A CALGARY MAN made a haggis from Alberta venison, liver, traditional toasted Scotch oats and special spices stuffed into a beef casing. There's nothing daft about that, except he then tried to shoot the haggis clear across the Bow River using his patented Haggis Launcher. And they say haggis never really 'took off' in Canada...

A US INVENTION designed to reduce food intake at meal times involved a fork that flashed up a green light at suitable intervals telling the eater when it was acceptable to take another mouthful. The inventors thought that this could significantly reduce the number of cases of obesity. It did not go down well.

Work

AN 1862 IDEA combined a hoe and gun in one handy tool; one end sporting a gun and the other a hoe. Farm workers would then be able to defend themselves quickly in the event of invasion from neighbouring enemies.

AN INVENTION FOR desk workers consists of a head rest that can be clamped to a desk and then extended to provide comfortable support to those who need to lean over their work for prolonged periods.

And finally...

A TIMELY INVENTION indeed was a watch telling you how long you have **left to live**. Simply calculate your life expectancy and programme it into the **timepiece**. It then counts down exactly how many years, months, days and hours you have left in this **mortal coil**. If the watch stops, watch out.

REALLY

DAFT

MARKETING

Even the big companies get it wrong sometimes. With all that money to spend on researching their products and markets you would have thought that the potential for cock-ups was small. But no. Have a look at some of these daft marketing mistakes and take comfort from the fact that no one is safe from the curse of human daftness.

CLAIROL INTRODUCED THE 'Mist Stick', a curling iron, into Germany only to find out that 'mist' is German slang for 'manure'.

ANOTHER LINGUISTIC OVERSIGHT ensured that Vicks failed to win German customers with its new cough drops. In their native tongue the name Vicks is pronounced 'ficks', which is German slang for sexual penetration.

'BIMBO DONUTS' ARE very popular in their native Mexico but did not receive a positive response in the US (the country that gave us *Baywatch*).

THE FRENCH DRINK 'Pschitt' is a popular brand of soda in Europe. For obvious reasons the name does not work well in English-speaking countries.

THE FIRST TINNED food was sold in 1812. The first tin-opener, however, didn't appear until 1860.

THE VAUXHALL NOVA was a non-starter in Spanish-speaking countries. *'No va'* means 'It does not go' in Spanish.

FORD HAD A similar translation problem in Brazil when its Pinto flopped. It turned out that *pinto* is Brazilian slang for 'small male genitalia'. Ford re-badged all the cars Corcel, which means horse.

WHEN PEPSI FIRST exported to Taiwan, their slogan was 'Come alive with the Pepsi Generation'. This was translated into Chinese rather too literally as 'Pepsi brings your ancestors back from the grave'.

COCA-COLA'S FIRST EXPORTS to China were given a name that had a similar pronunciation to the original – 'Ke-kou-ke-la'. Unfortunately the characters used meant 'bite the wax tadpole' (or 'female horse stuffed with wax' depending on the dialect), but thousands of signs had been printed before this was realised. A close phonetic equivalent, 'Ko-kou-ko-le', was eventually found that translated more favourably as 'happiness in the mouth'.

ALSO IN CHINA, the Kentucky Fried Chicken slogan 'finger-lickin' good' translated as 'eat your fingers off'.

COORS TRANSLATED ITS slogan 'Turn it loose' into Spanish where it was read as 'Suffer from diarrhoea'.

THE AMERICAN SLOGAN for Salem cigarettes, 'Salem – feeling free', was translated into the Japanese market as 'When smoking Salem, you will feel so refreshed that your mind seems to be free and empty'.

WHEN A RANGE of products called 'Big John' were launched in French-speaking parts of Canada, they were re-named as 'Gros Jos' until the manufacturers found out that the phrase, in slang, means 'big breasts'.

AN ITALIAN CAMPAIGN for Schweppes Tonic Water translated the name as 'Schweppes Toilet Water'.

SCANDINAVIAN VACUUM MANUFACTURER Electrolux failed to pay attention to US slang when they used the following in an American ad campaign: 'Nothing sucks like an Electrolux'.

A CHICKEN COMPANY'S slogan, 'It takes a tough man to make a tender chicken', was translated into Spanish as 'It takes a sexually stimulated man to make a chicken affectionate'. The company's owner was pictured next to one of his chickens with this slogan on billboards all over Mexico.

REALLY DAFT IDEAS

AN AMERICAN CLOTHING manufacturer printed T-shirts for the Spanish market to promote a visit by the Pope. Embarrassingly, instead of their shirts saying 'I saw the Pope' in Spanish, they actually boasted 'I saw the potato'.

AN AMERICAN BABY food manufacturer decided to export its products to **Africa** and used the same **baby picture** on the label that they used at home. When sales were not what they expected, they found out why... in Africa companies only put pictures on the label of what is actually **inside the tin**, since many people could not read.

REALLY

DAFT
STORIES

Our poor newsreaders. Day after day they are forced to tell us about dirty politicians, murderers at large and tragedy around the world. No wonder they look like they've been sucking lemons. If only their 6 o'clock bulletins consisted of the following true stories, which give the word 'tragic' a whole new meaning...

A SUCCESSFUL AUTHOR of children's books from Yorkshire was moving house and decided to burn some useless junk and clutter. It was only when he spotted a scorched page of his big-selling hit in bonfire ashes that he realised he had accidentally burned the original manuscript of his first book. Upon realising his error, he searched his house and found he'd also destroyed two later books. He could have sold the originals for £100,000.

A DELIVERYMAN IN West London received a £100 gift voucher from his employers, who decided it was time to reward him for his 12-year accident-free driving record. The man crashed his van two hours later.

EXPERTS HAVE STATED that they are prepared to pay £2 million to anyone who can find Julius Caesars autograph, though they admit that nobody knows what his signature looks like.

A NOT-SO-BRIGHT SOLDIER was crushed to death in his barrack room when he tied a hammock between two wall lockers. When he lay in the hammock, the lockers were pulled in on him, killing him.

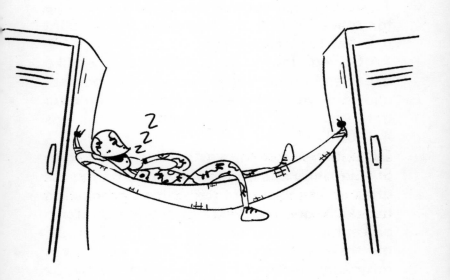

A GERMAN LAWYER set records after he earned more than £300,000 for less than an hour's work. The lawyer received the fee for sending a standard letter to the German tax office to correct an elderly client's tax bill. The letter pointed out that his client could not possibly have run up a 287 million euro tax bill on his 17,000 euro income from investments. The tax office agreed and amended the amount to a few thousand euros.

A German law, which no doubt seemed like a perfectly good idea when it was passed, allows lawyers to base their fee on the amount of the reduction. In this case the amount was 440,000 euros.

The lawyer's client was a 70 year old from St Augustin near Bonn, who was sent the bill after visiting his local tax office to make his tax declaration in 2001. He had put down an estimate on his earnings of 11,000 euros, but then corrected it to 17,000 – which was mistakenly entered into the computer by tax staff as an income of 1,100,017,000 euros.

The Jobcentre believe in the value of political correctness, but some may feel they have gone too far. A Hampshire businesswoman sent in an ad for 'hard-working' staff which they banned, saying it discriminated against the lazy. The 57-year-old woman was understandably perplexed. She had tried to place the ad for 'warehouse packers who must be hard-working and reliable', but was told that the word hard-working was unacceptable unless used with a clear job description.

A JORDANIAN MAN had been flirting with a woman in an Internet chat room for several months. Being a married man, he had assumed the online identity of Adnan, while the woman had described herself as an unmarried Muslim lady called Jamila whose cultural interests included reading. But when they finally met up at a bus station in Zarqa near Amman, he recognised his virtual girlfriend as his actual wife. He immediately shouted the Arabic words for 'I divorce thee' three times, effectively ending the marriage. The woman responded by calling him a liar before she fainted.

After catching her husband with another woman a Chinese wife negotiated with him that **he pay her** the equivalent of £6 for every hour he stayed away from home after midnight. This did not curb his **cheating ways**, however, and after paying his fine once he proceeded to produce a series of IOU notes to cover his dalliances. Fed up of this, his wife **filed for divorce** and at a court in Chongqing, central China, the judge granted her wish and also demanded that the man pay the IOU notes amounting to over £250.

A LETTER ADDRESSED to Adolf Hitler arrived at the German Parliament building after being sent from the UK. Addressed 'To Führer Adolf Hitler, Reichstag, German Parliament, Berlin, Germany', the letter was delayed due to a faulty address. Many felt that the postal service had displayed bad taste but a spokesperson said that it wasn't up to them to decide whether or not to deliver mail... even though the letter arrived more than 60 years after Hitler's death.

It's not wise to put the safety of imaginary friends before your own. A Frenchwoman proved this point when she was killed after her car crashed into a tree near Marseilles. She had been distracted from the road by the beeping of her pet Tamagotchi, attached to her key ring. Rather than let the little cyber pet die, she tried to save it and thus killed herself.

A MAN WAS train surfing in Australia and, although he was on a diesel train, the track merged with one used by electric trains. He slammed into the overhead power cables at some speed. Little trace was left of him.

IN ENGLAND, A foolish man died attempting to demonstrate his theory that railway power cables did not contain any current while the train was stationary.

AN ADVENTUROUS DRIVER decided to strap a JATO (Jet Assisted Take Off) unit to his car in an attempt to take flight. The Arizona man found a stretch of long, straight road and fired up his engine. Evidence from the scene of the incident suggests that the vehicle accelerated to full speed within five seconds with the car reaching up to 350 mph. The car remained on the road for a couple of miles at which point the driver attempted to brake, in so doing melting the brake pads and causing the tyres to explode. The car then finally became airborne… just in time for it to crash into the cliff directly ahead. Only small fragments of the driver were recovered from the scene.

REALLY DAFT IDEAS

A **DRUNKEN MAN** demonstrated why it is daft to walk near rail tracks when inebriated. Walking along a railroad on his way home he fell over and passed out with his left arm and left leg lying on the track. A train came along and severed them both. This is undoubtedly unfortunate enough, but almost exactly ten years later the same man again fell drunkenly onto a railway track and managed this time to lose his remaining arm and leg.

THREE BRAZILIANS WERE flying at low altitude in a plane when another plane flew close by. They decided it would be fun to 'drop a moonie' at the other plane, but in doing so they lost control of the plane and crashed. The three bodies were found inside the aircraft with their pants around their ankles.

WHEN TWO ITALIAN sailors arrived in Australia to compete for the America's Cup in 1986, they went out for a day to see a bit of bush country. A kangaroo jumped in front of their hire car and they couldn't avoid hitting him. They were shocked, thinking they had killed it, but not so shocked that they couldn't have some fun. One of them propped the carcass up against their vehicle, while the other dressed it up in an expensive Gucci blazer and took a photo. The kangaroo, which had merely been stunned, suddenly took off into the bush, taking with it the Gucci blazer plus the cash and passport in the pocket.

IN CAIRO, SIX people drowned when they got stuck down a well on a farm. An 18-year-old farmer, his sister, two brothers and two elderly farmers all drowned at the bottom of the fated well. The six bodies were later pulled out by the police along with the original cause of the carnage – a chicken, which had survived.

IN 1984, A Canadian farmer began renting out advertising space on his cows.

A man from Charlottesville, Virginia, was suspected of possessing a large haul of illegal drugs. Federal agents searched his house but could find no trace of the drugs or the man. They were just about to leave when they heard a sound coming from the fridge. Upon further investigation they found the man curled up inside. He would have escaped if not for his thirst, forcing him to open a can of fizzy drink.

WHILST DRIVING HOME one night, a man ran over a cat that was crossing the road. He pulled in, stepped outside to look for the cat, and found it lying at the side of the road. The impact had been quite hard, and he thought it kindest to put the moggy out of its misery. He took the steering lock from the car and clubbed the cat repeatedly on the head with it. Satisfied that the cat was truly dead, he continued his journey home. Later that night, some police officers knocked at his door investigating a report of animal cruelty. He told them what he had done, and the policemen checked the front of his car to verify the story. Embedded in the radiator grill they found the remains of the cat he had run over. The cat he had clubbed to death was, in fact, a perfectly healthy beast belonging to an elderly neighbour. Apparently this cat used to enjoy sleeping by the side of the road.

A RIVETER WORKING on a ship in the early twentieth century would sometimes ensure a watertight seal on the ship's outer hull by working in the narrow cavity between the outer and inner hulls to check the rivets were in place. On one occasion the riveter disappeared. The building of the ship was completed by his mystified colleagues, and served many years of active service. When finally the vessel was scrapped, workmen dismantling it found a skeleton and some riveting tools between the two hulls.

AN AMERICAN MAN and his friend went duck hunting with their dog. They drove up to a frozen lake in a brand new four wheel drive jeep and set about trying to make a hole in the ice in which they could float their decoys. They decided that the best method to create the hole was to use dynamite, so they lit a stick and threw it out onto the frozen lake. Their dog, however, mistook the act for a game and ran out to collect the stick of dynamite for his owners. The two men were understandably concerned when the dog came bounding towards them clutching his prize. Thinking quickly, one of the men decided to shoot the dog but, the gun being full of duck shot, the dog was not seriously hurt and continued, confused, to approach the men. Firing again, the man frightened the dog so much that he had to take cover... underneath the brand new jeep. A couple of seconds later the dynamite exploded, and neither dog nor jeep ever went hunting again.

IN A SOUTH African hospital staff noticed that all the patients who spent the night in one particular intensive care room died without fail. The situation was monitored but doctors could find no reason for this anomaly. All the furniture was changed, the air conditioning was checked and all medical equipment thoroughly serviced. Despite these efforts the next patient to stay in the room suffered the same fate as those who had gone before. Suspecting criminal involvement doctors stepped up their case and kept a 24-hour watch on the room. They soon found the cause. A cleaner had been coming into the room every night and using a floor polishing machine. As there was only one plug socket in the room, the cleaner had unwittingly been unplugging the life support machine each time she wanted to polish the floor.

Two animal rights protesters decided to free pigs from a slaughterhouse in Germany. The two thousand pigs stampeded, trampling the protesters to death.

A DAFT CAR burglar tried using the butt of his gun as a club to smash a windscreen. The gun went off and shot him in the abdomen, killing him.

A 47-YEAR-OLD MAN was woken one night by the sound of the phone ringing by the side of his bed. When he reached for it he picked up his revolver instead, which he imprudently kept next to the phone. When he put it to his ear, he shot himself dead.

TWO COUSINS DECIDED to play a game of Russian roulette using a semi automatic pistol. The tradition is for the game to be played using a revolver in which all bullet chambers are empty except one, giving the players some chance of survival. Tragically for one of the cousins, a semi automatic pistol will always fire, even with one bullet.

WHILE ON HOLIDAY in South Africa's Kruger Park, two **Japanese tourists** came across a pair of sleeping lions. Disappointed that the beasts were not doing anything more interesting, one of the tourists climbed out of their jeep and tried to **liven them up** by giving them a little kick and shouting in their ear. The tourist **was successful** in his quest but was unable to take any pictures before his demise.

A MAN FROM Focsany in Romania unwittingly lost both his wife and his mistress in one day after trying to treat them both with a surprise gift. He bought two identical gold necklaces and had a special message engraved on each one for his respective lovers. Heading off to work one morning the man later received a call from his wife's lawyer saying that she was filing for divorce. The man had foolishly mixed up the gifts and the women both found out about his cheating ways.

REALLY DAFT IDEAS

AFTER SPENDING A few hours drinking together a group of male friends thought it might be fun to play some 'men's games'. So, stripping off, they began to hit each other over the head with frozen turnips. Things moved up a notch when one of the group grabbed a chainsaw and chopped off part of his foot. Strangely impressed, another member of the group took the chainsaw and with the shout, 'Watch this, then!' proceeded to take a swing at his neck, cutting his head clean off.

More than sixty years ago, a Hollywood actress called Lupe Velez tried to kill herself by overdosing on sleeping pills. She didn't take enough, however, and rushed for the bathroom feeling violently sick. As she entered the bathroom she slipped on the tiled floor and fell head first into the toilet, where she drowned.

AN UNFORTUNATE YORKSHIREMAN dropped his car keys down a drain after he had spent an evening drinking in a remote pub. He could see them glinting on some dry leaves inside the drain, so he lifted the cover up and leaned in. The keys were just a little too far to reach, so he leaned in further and promptly fell in, head first. When it started to rain a few hours later the man was still trapped. Unable to attract help, he drowned when the drain filled.

THE LOS ANGELES *Times* unwittingly juxtaposed an ad banner demanding that readers 'Follow that Fool!' above a photo of a sombre Zairian man being marched to his death by rebel soldiers just moments before his execution.

AT NEW YORK City's 'LMAK projects' gallery in February 2004, artist Emily Katrencik gnawed sections of the drywall separating the gallery's exhibition space from the director's office for 30 minutes a day, 5 days a week. The artist claimed to prefer cast concrete because it has a more metallic flavour.

A PSYCHOLOGY STUDENT rented out her spare room to a man in order to nag him constantly and study his reactions. After weeks of being nagged, he finally snapped and beat her repeatedly, leaving her brain-dead.

A WOMAN ENTERING her kitchen was horrified to see her husband shaking violently with what looked like a wire running from his body towards the electric kettle. Thinking he was being electrocuted, she attempted to jolt him away from the source of the current by hitting him hard with a plank of wood from the garden. The impact fractured his arm in two places, which annoyed him greatly as he had only been listening to a personal stereo.

A MAN RETURNING from his holiday in Cuba was guilty of a right cock-up. During his holiday the man had spent much of his time in the local brothels where he had been introduced to erectile cream for the first time. Upon returning home he was admitted to hospital complaining of a permanent erection and swollen testicles. It turned out that the man had become so addicted to the cream that he had ignored advice to use the cream sparingly and had instead applied it liberally every day. Doctors said that the man should make the most of his erection as it was likely to be his last.

A RIGHT PAIR of tits caused a string of strange accidents when a woman decided to flash her breasts at her husband as he was leaving for work. A passing taxi driver saw this, and crashed into the corner of an adjacent dental surgery. Inside this building, a dental technician was cleaning a man's teeth when the noise of the crash made her jump, causing her to tear the man's gums with a cleaning pick. In shock, the man instinctively clamped his teeth down and bit off two of her fingers. The woman who had flashed her breasts was then struck by a piece of the damaged dental surgery falling onto her head.

A daft man was admitted to hospital with a shotgun wound to his leg. The reason for his predicament, he explained, was that he had seen a spider crawling up his leg, so he shot it.

REALLY DAFT IDEAS

SEVERAL DRUNKEN MEN were walking across a high bridge in the early hours of the morning when one of them mentioned that a friend of his had once bungee-jumped from the bridge. With inebriated enthusiasm, the men decided to have a go themselves. Unfortunately none had brought any bungee rope with them. Not to be discouraged, one of them suggested using a coil of cable that lay nearby. One end of the cable was duly tied around his leg and the other was secured to the bridge. He bravely dived off the side of the bridge, plunging 40 feet until the cable tightened and pulled his foot off at the ankle. He survived the fall into the icy waters below, but his foot was never recovered.

REALLY DAFT STORIES

WHILE BOASTING ABOUT the safety features of the new windows in his Toronto office, a 39-year-old lawyer threw himself against the glass to startle his visitor. He achieved this (and more) when the glass shattered and he plunged 24 floors to his death.

AN AMATEUR RADIO operator was building himself an 80-foot radio transmitter mast, using a large quantity of heavy tools and equipment in order to complete the top. When he had finished it seemed like a good idea to **lower the items** to the ground using a pulley. He climbed down, secured a rope at ground level, then climbed back up to load the tools into a barrel. He then climbed down once again and untied the rope, holding on tightly with the intention of letting the barrel fall slowly under his control.

However, he had **miscalculated the weight** of the tools in the barrel – they weighed almost twice as much as he did. So surprised was he at being yanked upwards by the weight of the falling barrel that he forgot to let go of the rope. Halfway up the tower, he crashed into the barrel coming down, fracturing his **skull and collarbone**. He didn't stop, though, and continued rising until his knuckles hit the pulley. Despite the pain, he managed to hold onto the rope.

When the barrel hit the ground, the bottom fell out of it, releasing all its contents. Suddenly he weighed a great deal more than the barrel, and fell rapidly. Halfway down, he **met the barrel** coming up, fracturing his ankles. This impact slowed him down so that when he fell onto the pile of tools he only broke 3 vertebrae.

As he lay on the tools, in **great pain**, he finally let go of the rope, causing the empty barrel to fall on him from 80 feet. He survived.

A CANADIAN POLICE officer thought he would play a practical joke on a fellow officer at a firing range. He waited around a corner in the locker room and jumped out to frighten his colleague. The joke worked... his colleague was so shocked that he pulled his gun and shot the officer in the chest.

AN ELECTRICITY WORKMAN broke the basic safety rules when he needed to pee but didn't want to climb down to ground level or even back to the pylon. He was working on the cable itself, which is harmless provided you don't make contact with the ground. This is why birds don't get electrocuted when they sit on electricity cables. But this man decided to open his flies and take a leak from where he was. The stream of urine made contact with the earth and he was fried.

WHEN WORKING ON a sloping roof it makes sense to tie yourself to something secure, such as a chimney, in case you slip. An American man did just this, except that as he had no chimney he chose to tie the rope to his car which was parked on the other side of the house. He tied the knots meticulously, one around the car's bumper and the other around his waist, and made sure there was enough slack to allow him to work but not enough to fall very far should he slip. The only aspect in which he erred was in neglecting to tell his wife... she got into the car and drove off. Fortunately she had only driven a few metres before she noticed something was dragging behind her, and he was not seriously injured.

An American police officer was demonstrating to his colleagues why it is dangerous to holster a gun with your finger on the trigger. His demonstration turned out to be a little too realistic – he shot himself in the leg and bled to death. Two nights later, another officer was demonstrating how his colleague had shot himself, and the same thing happened again. He tried to drive himself to the hospital, but passed out from blood loss and was killed in the subsequent crash.

IN 1875, THE Director of the United States Patent Office resigned and recommended that the entire Patent Office be closed down as, he said, there was nothing left to be invented.

JUST ONE YEAR later, in Britain, the Post Office rejected the concept of the telephone on the grounds that most people had access to small boys who could deliver messages for them.

Always read the label: a French fashion model made a rather hair-raising faux pas when she accidentally used her bald-headed husband's new hair-restoring cream. Instead of the firmer breasts she was expecting, the unfortunate mademoiselle had great wads of hair growing from her assets.

A 25-YEAR-OLD AMERICAN man was charged with being a stowaway after he tried to save money on a trip home to see his parents in Texas. The man was reluctant to pay the airfare and, as he worked as a shipping clerk, thought it would be easier to pack himself into a shipping crate and mail himself home. Upon delivery to his parents' doorstep the man pushed himself out of the box and shook hands with the startled delivery driver. The driver immediately called the police and after a lengthy investigation the young man was charged for his crime.

IN AN EFFORT to continue its perfect, five-year-long safety record, a company showed its workers a film aimed at encouraging the use of safety goggles on the job. Unfortunately the film's depiction of gory industrial accidents was so graphic that twenty-five workers suffered minor injuries in their rush to leave the screening room, thirteen others fainted, and one man required seven stitches after he cut his head falling off a chair.

A **FRENCHMAN STRUGGLED** somewhat whilst trying to kill himself. He stood at the top of a high cliff, tied a noose around his head and secured the other end to a wooden stake. To make sure nothing was left to chance, he then drank some poison and set fire to himself. As if this wasn't enough, he even tried to shoot himself in the head. But he was a poor shot... the bullet missed him, and instead cut the rope in half. He fell into the sea, where the water put out the fire and the sudden cold made him vomit up his poison. He was rescued from the sea, but later died in hospital from exposure.

A COUPLE HAD an unusual marriage ceremony in the village of Ceres, South Africa when family and friends decided to go ahead with the wedding despite the fact that the pregnant bride had been murdered by her fiancé, who had then killed himself.

IN AN OTTAWA club, an employee turned up for her day's work, even though she had been fired the day before. Disgruntled and frustrated, the woman dumped bags of tuna in the club's cloakroom and champagne rooms, covering the tables, chairs and walls. Not satisfied with her fish fit, she then emptied two small canisters of pepper spray near the bar. She did not get her job back.

A US FARMER bought water beds for his herd of cows in his quest to bump up productivity. He joins farmers around the world who say such bovine pampering pays off. He began experimenting with 15 specially made water beds but is ordering 80 more for his 1,600 cows in Oregon's Willamette Valley.

OFFICIALS IN ZHONGDIAN, south-western China, have renamed their impoverished county Shangri-La, predicting the change will draw hordes of tourists seeking paradise. The county's name change was approved by China's cabinet.

BELIEVING THAT ALCOHOL was the root of all evil and that Prohibition would put an end to crime, some towns in the US actually sold their jails.

IN ITALY, TICKETS for the first commercial flight to Mars went on sale with assurances that it was the latest holiday destination and would allow tourists to discover a whole new culture. More than 600 would-be space travellers paid £6,000 each, netting the con men an out-of-this-world figure of £4 million.

IN THE MIDDLE Ages, there was a law in England which stated that any condemned man who could withdraw his head from the gibbet (a forerunner to the guillotine) in between the time when the blade was released to when it hit the bottom, and then run to a nearby town, would be pardoned. One man achieved this feat, and took great pleasure in boasting about it for years afterwards. His story became so tiresome that people started to think he had made it up. The man therefore decided to prove his story by putting his neck under the gibbet once more. He never told the story again.

THE BEATLES WERE turned down by a number of record companies before they finally secured a deal. A representative from one of these companies explained their reasoning: they believed guitar-based groups were on their way out.

IN AUSTRALIA A man was diagnosed with lead poisoning after he ate three feet of electrical cable in one day. He claimed that it had a sweet and enjoyable taste and that he got a buzz from the experience.

A convicted murderer was released in Argentina after his 'victim' turned up alive and well. The man, from Tucuman, had maintained his innocence after his arrest but was found guilty by a local judge and sent to Villa Urquiza prison. The 'dead man' was then spotted alive on the streets of Tucuman by the convict's sister; he told the police he had moved to another town to try his luck and had no idea people thought he was dead.

REALLY

DAFT

ROBBERS

(AND OTHER REALLY DAFT CRIMINALS)

There have been many cases of the criminal mastermind that have grabbed all our attention. Al Capone, the Biggs brothers and Lucky Luciano conjure up exciting images of a world of fast living and glamorous women. They lived like kings in the underworld and continue to fascinate us today, years after their crimes were committed. The collection of daft criminals you are about to meet, on the other hand, managed to put themselves under the spotlight for all the wrong reasons.

REALLY DAFT ROBBERS

A MAN IN America decided that a great way to rob a bank would be to use the drive through. After all he would already be in his getaway car. He pulled up to the window and handed the cashier a note demanding money. The cashier contained her laughter long enough to call the police and the suspect was soon apprehended.

A DAFT CRIMINAL was able to rob a bank and make a clean getaway. It all went downhill from there, though, as he returned to the same bank the following day and tried to deposit the stolen money into his bank account.

AFTER SCHEMING FOR some time an English bank robber thought he had planned the perfect job. He had even found a reliable getaway driver. Unfortunately, as the robber fled the bank, he was run over by that same driver.

DURING A TRIAL for possession of drugs, the defence claimed that their client had been searched without a warrant. The prosecutor pointed out that a warrant wasn't necessary when a suspect had a bulge in their jacket that might have been a gun. The defendant happened to be wearing the same jacket in court that day, and handed it over to the judge so that he could see for himself that it wasn't a gun. The judge looked in the inside pocket and found a bulbous packet of cocaine. Unable to control his laughter, he had to call a recess.

Six men charged with attempting Britain's biggest cash robbery managed to burn ten per cent of their haul. The prosecuting barrister said in court that the group had forced a security van, carrying over £10 million, into a wooded area. The group then used high-powered torches to open it. The torches set off a blaze that turned over £1 million into ashes and caused the men to flee for their safety.

AN AMERICAN WHO robbed two men at gunpoint in their homes dropped his wallet as he left and then called police to ask if they found the wallet. They said they had. They asked him to come down to the station and claim it. He did.

A PATIENT ROBBER went into a bank and waited in the queue. Before he got to the cashier he put on a ski mask and pulled out his gun. He then waited behind other customers for several more minutes before attempting to rob the bank.

REALLY DAFT ROBBERS

A HOPEFUL CRIMINAL spent several days casing a Boston bank and thought he knew just the right time to commit his crime. As he approached the cashier he shouted, 'This is a hold-up, nobody move!' What he didn't know was that the next five customers in the queue were FBI agents on their lunch break. He had failed to take note of the FBI office just down the street from the bank.

A HUNGRY US fugitive was caught out when he was tricked into coming back across the border from Canada. After living rough for several weeks, he was offered the chance of a free meal at a US diner by a scorned ex lover and was promptly arrested.

A PAIR OF robbers entered a record shop nervously waving revolvers. The first one shouted, 'Nobody move!' When his partner moved, the startled first bandit shot him.

REALLY DAFT ROBBERS

IN THE US kidnappers sent a photograph of their captive to his family. The victim was seen holding up a newspaper. It was not that day's edition and, in fact, bore a prominent headline relating to Nixon's trip to China. This was pointed out to the kidnappers in a subsequent phone call. They responded by sending a new photograph showing an up-to-date newspaper. The victim, however, did not appear in the picture. When this too was challenged, the kidnappers became peevish and insisted that a photograph be sent to them showing all the people at the victim's house holding different issues of *Success* magazine. They provided a mailing address and were immediately apprehended. They later admitted to FBI agents they did not understand the principle involved in the photograph/newspaper concept.

Police in Los Angeles had some luck with a robbery suspect who was unable to control himself during a line-up. When detectives asked each man in the line-up to repeat the words 'Give me all your money or I'll shoot', the robber shouted, 'That's not what I said!'

A MAN WAS arrested for trying to hold up a Bank of America branch without a weapon. He used a thumb and a finger to simulate a gun but, carelessly, he failed to keep his hand in his pocket.

A GERMAN WOMAN seeking the ultimate in skin lotion decided that she would bathe in the milk of a camel. So she **stole a camel** from the local zoo and transported it back to her house, where **she realised** that the camel's name was a distinctly masculine-sounding 'Otto'.

REALLY DAFT ROBBERS

A MAN WAS charged with holding up a shoe store and stealing about £50 in shoes. At his trial the prosecutor asked to see his shoes. He was wearing the boots he stole, with the tags still on.

A YOUNG MAN walked into a shop with a shotgun and demanded all the money from the till. After the shop assistant put the money in a bag, a bottle of Scotch on the shelf behind the counter caught the robber's eye and he told the cashier to put that in the bag as well.

The cashier refused, not believing the man to be over the minimum age. The robber took his driving licence out of his wallet and gave it to the assistant, who looked it over, agreed that the man was old enough and put the Scotch in the bag.

The robber then ran from the shop with his loot. The shop assistant promptly called the police and gave them the name and address of the robber.

REALLY DAFT ROBBERS

A 19-YEAR-OLD MAN was charged with bank robbery in the state of Virginia, USA. The man was easily caught after he made a series of daft errors.

After successfully leaving the bank with his loot the man suddenly realised that he had left his note of demands in the bank and returned to retrieve it. Leaving the bank for the second time it was not long before he noticed that he had left the keys to his getaway car in the bank as well. Not wishing to go back in again, the man decided to walk home from the scene of the crime.

Returning to his house the man then informed his housemate, whose car he had borrowed, that his car had been stolen. The housemate promptly called the police and it was not long before they pieced together the details of the crime and arrested the man.

AN AMERICAN BANK robber was easily caught by surveillance cameras. He thought rubbing citric acid on his face would blur the picture. It didn't.

WHEN A MAN tried to commit a robbery in the US, there were several indications that this was his first offence. The shop he tried to rob happened to be a gun shop, and it was also full of customers, many of whom carried their own guns. There was a police car parked outside, and a uniformed officer was inside, standing next to the counter. The robber saw the police officer and announced a hold-up, firing some shots into the ceiling. The officer and the shopkeeper both returned fire, killing him.

A WOMAN WAS arrested in Florida for attempting to rob a motel. She was armed with only an electric chainsaw, which was not plugged in.

A BELGIAN MAN suspected of robbing a jewellery store in Liège insisted he was innocent. His foolproof alibi was that he was at the local school at the time – breaking in. Police then arrested him for his actual crime.

TWO ROBBERS TRIED to pull the front off a cash machine by attaching a chain from the machine to the bumper of their car. Instead of pulling the front panel off the machine, though, they pulled the bumper off their car. They became nervous and quickly drove off, leaving the chain still attached to the machine, with the bumper still attached to the chain, and with the car's number plate attached to the bumper.

A ROBBER WALKED into a shop and demanded all the money in the till. The shopkeeper handed him the money and the robber left... forgetting his wallet, which was on the counter with his ID inside.

WHEN A CONVICTED robber negotiated a deal to pay compensation in lieu of serving a few months in prison, he paid the court with a forged cheque.

A GROUP OF employees at a large aerospace company used their lunch hour to do some banking; more accurately, to rob a bank near their place of work. Returning to the plant after lunch they were confident that they had got away with their crime. Sadly, they had forgotten to remove their ID badges during the robbery.

A CROOK FROM the US was caught out when he tried to rob the First Community Bank in Fargo. He entered the bank pretending to be a customer and handed the cashier a list of demands he had quickly written down. The cashier gave the man what he asked for and he left the bank with his loot. After searching the area police had no leads, but on further inspection it was noticed that the man had written his demands on his own bank deposit slip. Travelling to the man's house police were able to arrest the perpetrator with ease.

A ROBBER BURST into a shop brandishing a gun and announced a hold-up. Before anyone could get a good look at his face he cleverly pulled a bag over his head, and only then realised he had forgotten to put any eyeholes in the bag.

Another bank robber broke into a bank's basement through a street-level window, cutting himself up quite badly in the process. He then found that he had no access to any of the bank's money from where he was, and that he couldn't climb back outside through the same window. He was bleeding so much from his injuries that he had to phone the emergency services to rescue him.

REALLY DAFT ROBBERS

AN OVERWEIGHT MAN from Washington entered a bank and demanded money from the cashiers. Leaving the bank with his extra load the twenty-stone man made his getaway on foot, as he had neglected to arrange the use of a vehicle. Unfortunately the unfit robber soon tired and was easily arrested by security staff when he paused to take a break.

A MAN ATTEMPTED to rob an antiques shop. Having ransacked the till in the middle of the night, he spotted an old brass diving helmet in the shop and couldn't resist trying it on. The helmet got stuck, so he decided to make his escape with it still on his head. He stepped outside into the road and was run over by a lorry.

A MAN WIELDING a knife attempted to open a shop's till. Failing to **achieve his aim**, he ripped the till from the counter and began running towards the exit but didn't get very far as **the till was bolted** to the wall via an electrical cord. He was jerked back and collapsed in a heap on the floor. Frustrated, he tried to cut the cord, which was still plugged in, using his knife. This caused showers of sparks to fly about his head and hands. Eventually he managed to **stagger out** of the shop carrying the cash register, but was caught soon after by police.

REALLY DAFT ROBBERS

A MAN WALKED into a Burger King one morning at 7.50 a.m., flashed a gun and demanded cash. The server turned him down because, he said, he couldn't open the till without a food order. When the man ordered onion rings, the server said they weren't available for breakfast. The man, frustrated, walked away.

WHEN TWO PETROL station workers refused to hand over their takings to a drunk and rather dim robber, the man threatened to call the police. They still refused, so the robber called the police and was arrested.

FIREFIGHTERS HAD TO knock down a chimney to rescue a burglar who had got himself stuck while attempting to enter a house in Buenos Aires. The man was arrested after being freed from the chimney.

REALLY DAFT ROBBERS

AN AMERICAN MAN was arrested for forgery after going into a bank and presenting a suspicious looking cheque to a cashier. After making a few security checks the bank staff called the police while the man waited in the banking hall, blissfully ignorant that the police were on their way. Once arrested the police noted that, even if the man had fled, he would have been easily caught because he had given the cashier his real driving licence details.

AN UNIDENTIFIED MAN in Buenos Aires pushed his wife out of an eighth-floor window, but his plan to kill her failed when she became entangled in some power cables below. Seeing that she was still alive, the man jumped and tried to land on top of her. He missed.

THIEVES BROKE INTO a warehouse in the US by crossing a metal bridge and then blew it up... having forgotten it was their only means of escape.

REALLY DAFT ROBBERS

A MAN ATTEMPTED to siphon fuel from a motor home parked on a US street and got much more than he bargained for. Police arrived at the scene to find a poorly man curled up next to the motor home near spilled sewage. A police spokesman said that the man admitted trying to steal fuel but plugged his hose into the motor home's sewage tank by mistake.

UPON ENTERING A bank a would-be robber tripped on the doorstep, which caused his mask to fall from his face. Then his foot caught under the doormat and he slid across the floor towards the counter. At this point the dazed crook got to his feet, waved his fake gun in the air, and declared, 'This is a stuff-up!'

A group of English robbers hired what they thought was a suitable candidate to be their getaway driver. As they came running out of the bank with their haul the driver stalled the car in a panic. After several more attempts to get the car moving, police arrived and arrested the gang. It turned out that the driver did not have a licence and had in fact never even driven a car before.

REALLY DAFT ROBBERS

In Detroit a 21-year-old man was arrested by police for a robbery that he had carried out two years previously. His crime was revealed when he approached two police officers who were showing their criminal location equipment to a group of children. Intrigued, the man asked how the system worked and gave his information to the officers to put into the computer. He was immediately arrested as the screen showed that he was wanted for the robbery that had taken place in Missouri.

AN AMERICAN MAN thought his insurance company made a mistake when they agreed to insure his box of rare and expensive cigars against fire. He smoked all of the cigars within a month, and filed a claim against the insurance company stating that he had lost them in a series of small fires.

The insurance company refused to pay out, claiming that he had consumed the cigars in the normal fashion. He went on to sue them, and won his case. This unlikely victory was due to the fact that the insurance company had agreed that the cigars were insurable against fire, and had not defined what was an 'acceptable' form of fire. Rather than bothering to appeal, which would have been costly for the insurance company, it agreed to pay the man $15,000 to compensate for the loss of the cigars.

However, the company then had the man arrested on 24 counts of arson, and was able to use his own insurance claim and testimony from the previous case as evidence against him. They won the case, and the man was sentenced to 24 consecutive one-year prison terms.

AN AMERICAN MAN pretending to have a gun kidnapped a motorist and forced him to drive to two different automated cash machines. The kidnapper then proceeded to withdraw money from his *own* bank accounts. Police later tracked him down without too much trouble.

AN ESCAPED CONVICT was eventually caught by police after a car chase reaching speeds of up to 150 mph. He explained that he was driving so fast to try and get far enough ahead of the police to allow himself the space to turn round and stop. This explanation did not help his case.

A MAN STOLE £75,000 worth of pigs to help pay for breast implants for his favourite stripper at a club. He got ten years in prison.

A YOUNG THIEF tried to steal a handbag from an old lady who was sitting inside a photo booth waiting for the machine to take her picture. Not only did he leave empty-handed, having failed to wrench the bag from her grip, but he also appeared very clearly in one of her photos, for which the police were very grateful.

REALLY DAFT IDEAS

IN FRANCE TWO would-be criminals thought that it might be a good idea to break into a bank from an adjacent building. They planned to drill through the wall into the vault of the bank, but after hours of deafening labour they succeeded only in arriving in the middle of the staff toilets.

REALLY DAFT ROBBERS

WALKING INTO HIS local Bank of America branch a US man wrote out his demands on the back of a credit slip. It read, 'This iz a stikkup. Put all yor muny in this bag.' The man continued to wait in line for several minutes but became worried that one of the other customers may have seen him write the note. In a panic he quickly left the bank and headed over the road to try his luck elsewhere.

After waiting for several minutes there, he finally handed his demands to the cashier. She quickly realised the extent of his intellect and advised him that because his demands were written on a Bank of America slip she couldn't help him. He could either fill out a new slip or go back to the other bank.

A little deflated, the man headed back over the road while the cashier promptly called the police. They arrested the man shortly afterwards – still queuing at the Bank of America.

A WOMAN WAS arrested after a mechanic reported to police that 18 packages of marijuana were packed in the engine compartment of her car which she had brought to the mechanic for an oil change. Apparently she didn't realise that the mechanic would have to raise the bonnet to change the oil.

A MAN WALKED into a police station and dropped a bag of cocaine on the counter. He informed the desk sergeant that it was sub-standard cut, and asked that the person who sold it to him be arrested immediately.

A **COMPANY CALLED** 'Guns For Hire' that specialised in staging gunfights for Western movies received a call from a woman who wanted to have her husband killed. She got a life sentence.

MISCHIEVOUS POLICE INTERROGATED a criminal suspect by placing a metal colander on his head and connecting it with wires to a photocopier. The message 'He's lying' was placed in the photocopier, and the police pressed the copy button each time they thought the suspect wasn't telling the truth. Believing the 'lie detector' was working, the suspect confessed.

A TERRORIST SENT a letter bomb but failed to put sufficient postage on it. The bomb was delivered back to him marked 'Return to sender'... and, rather daftly, he opened it.

A LOS ANGELES man who later said he was 'tired of walking' stole a steamroller and led police on a 5 mph, chase until an officer stepped aboard and brought the vehicle to a stop.

A MAN WAS sentenced to two years in prison for **faking his death** three times to beat drink driving charges. The criminal was first arrested in 1991, but an official-looking death certificate sent to authorities said he had died in a Los Angeles road accident, and **the case was dismissed**. In 1994, he was arrested again and sent in another death certificate. A year later, he was again arrested and supposedly **died this time** of 'denzor hemorrhagic fever' in Africa. There is no such disease.

THREE AMERICAN MEN were determined to rob a bank but as they tried to enter they got stuck in the revolving doors. After going away for a rethink the men returned and demanded $10,000 from bank staff. They were only greeted by laughter, however, as the staff and customers remembered their first attempt and thought the whole thing was a practical joke.

The robbers, unaware of this, thought that the laughter was caused by the high figure they were demanding and lowered their request to $1,000. This did not work either and it was not long before the men were asking for just one dollar each. At this point one of the men angrily jumped on the counter and pulled out a gun, only to fall and break his leg. The other two tried to escape – but again got stuck in the revolving doors.

A WOMAN WHO allegedly stole £700 worth of clothing from a department store chose the wrong place to hide when she slipped away from security guards. According to police the 19-year-old jumped into the parked car of two off-duty policemen in an ill-fated attempt to evade capture.

A MAN WAS injured in the US after he attempted to replace a fuse in his car with a rifle bullet which happened to be a perfect fit. When electricity heated the bullet it went off and shot him in the knee.

AFTER KNOCKING OUT the driver of a security van a 33-year-old US man fled the scene with four large bags of money. Unfortunately each bag contained $800 in coins and weighed in at around 12kg. The weight of his crime slowed the man down and police had no trouble catching up with the exhausted crook.

REALLY DAFT ROBBERS

A LAWYER DEFENDING a man accused of burglary claimed that it was only the client's arm that had actually committed the offence and as such his whole body should not be punished. The judge agreed and sentenced the arm to a year in prison, leaving it up to the defendant whether or not he accompanied it. The defendant smiled. With his lawyer's assistance he detached his artificial limb, laid it on the bench, and walked out.

A US MOTHER always wanted her sons to succeed in life. This continued into their adulthood. Her sons grew up to be firemen, and she intentionally set fires to help their careers. After five fires in one month she was arrested for arson.

REALLY DAFT LAWS

Professionals in the field of law study and train for several years to become experts in their subject. They are conversant in affidavits, *sub silentio* and *talis qualis*, and we can sleep at night thanks to their criminal justice system. You may wonder, though, if some were *non compos mentis* when they came up with these daft laws.

REALLY DAFT LAWS

ALL BATHTUBS MUST be located outdoors, not in the house.

Virginia, USA

ALL MALES OVER the age of 14 are to practise longbow for two hours a week under the supervision of the local clergy.

England

IT IS AGAINST the law for a drunk to be in possession of a cow.

Scotland

IT IS ILLEGAL to shoot a Welsh person with a bow and arrow, except after midnight within the city walls.

Chester, England

A WOMAN MAY only be topless in public if she is an assistant in a tropical fish store.

UK

REALLY DAFT LAWS

IT IS LEGAL to shoot a Scotsman with a bow and arrow, except on Sundays.

York, England

IF TWO TRAINS meet on the same track, neither shall proceed until the other has passed.

Kansas, USA

CITIZENS ARE FORBIDDEN to greet each other by 'putting one's thumb to the nose and wiggling the fingers'.

New York, USA

PERSONS CLASSIFIED AS 'ugly' are not permitted to walk down any street.

California, USA

IT IS AN offence to shower naked.

Florida, USA

IT IS AGAINST the law for frogs to croak after 11 p.m.

Memphis, Tennessee, USA

THE PENALTY FOR jumping off a building is death.

New York, USA

MEN AND WOMEN over the age of 18 must reveal at least one missing tooth when smiling.

Arizona, USA

IT IS ILLEGAL for a vehicle without a driver to exceed 60 miles per hour.

California, USA

A DRIVER MAY not be blindfolded while operating a vehicle.

Alabama, USA

DOMINOES CANNOT BE played on Sunday.

Alabama, USA

IT IS AGAINST the law to sing in a public place while dressed in a swimsuit.

Miami, USA

IT IS ILLEGAL to wear a fake moustache that causes laughter in church.

Alabama, USA

IT IS ILLEGAL for animals to mate publicly within 1,500 feet of a tavern, school or place of worship.

California, USA

IT IS CONSIDERED a misdemeanour if you shoot at any kind of game from a moving vehicle, unless the target is a whale.

Tennessee, USA

UNMARRIED WOMEN ARE banned from parachuting on Sunday or they shall risk arrest, fine and/or jailing.

Florida, USA

MEN ARE FORBIDDEN to be seen publicly in any kind of strapless gown.

Florida, USA

IT IS ILLEGAL to have sexual relations with a porcupine.

Florida, USA

SKATEBOARDING WITHOUT A licence is illegal.

Florida, USA

WITH REGARDS TO sexual intercourse, only the missionary position is legal.

Florida, USA

HANGING CLOTHES ON a clothesline can only be carried out after purchasing the correct licence.

New York, USA

IT IS A crime to throw a ball at someone's head for fun.

New York, USA

WHILE STANDING, A person is not permitted to take more than three sips of beer at a time.

Texas, USA

IT IS AGAINST the law to shoot a buffalo from the second storey of a hotel.

Texas, USA

A RECENTLY PASSED anticrime law requires criminals to give their victims 24 hours' notice, either orally or in writing, and to explain the nature of the crime to be committed.

Texas, USA

IT IS ILLEGAL to make beer at home. For this reason, the entire *Encyclopaedia Britannica* is banned as it contains a formula for this activity.

Texas, USA

THE PENALTY FOR flirting is $25. In particular, men are prohibited from turning around on any city street and looking 'at a woman in that way'. A second conviction for such an offence results in the violating male being forced to wear a 'pair of horse-blinders' wherever and whenever he goes outside for a stroll.

USA

IF AN ELEPHANT is left tied to a parking meter, the parking fee has to be paid just as it would for a vehicle.

Florida, USA

A HOUSING LAW states that tenants in public housing must not die without giving at least 30 days' notice.

Gloucester, England

WHAT THE VICTORIANS DIDN'T DO FOR US

ALASTAIR WILLIAMS

£7.99

Paperback

Did you know that washing your teeth with charcoal was once believed to make them whiter? That ladies were encouraged to drink vinegar to appear pale and delicate?

From the strange to the downright unsavoury, learn what the Victorians *didn't* do for us.

REALLY RUDE JOKES

B. A. STARD

£4.99

Paperback

The crudest classrooms, the sleaziest bars and the smuttiest office e-mails have been dredged for this bumper collection of dirty jokes – so fucking funny you'll piss yourself.

Raunchily rude and sensationally lewd, *Really Rude Jokes* is the ultimate bad influence for all gutter-dwelling minds.

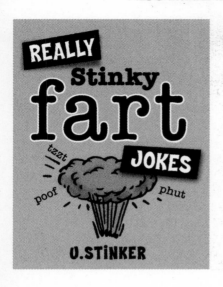

www.summersdale.com